The Book
of Ogham

POCKET EDITION

Published from
The Joshua Free Imprint – JFI Publications
Mardukite Borsippa HQ, San Luis Valley, Colorado
Founding Church of Mardukite Zuism,
Mardukite Academy & Systemology Society
for religious and educational purposes only.

The book of Ogham

A DRUID'S GUIDE TO THE CELTIC TREE ORACLE

Based on the work by Joshua Free
Edited by Rowen Gardner

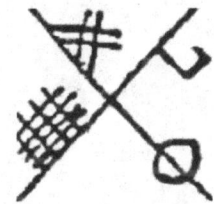

THE JOSHUA FREE IMPRINT
JFI PUBLICATIONS

© 2023, JOSHUA FREE

ISBN : 979-8-9871249-5-6

Premiere Paperback Edition — *April 2023*

Mardukite D-Series Supplement

mardukite.com

The Secret Language of Trees—Revealed!

Learn the Secret Language of Trees with a
treasury of Druidic knowledge and esoteric lore
supporting a Celtic Tree Oracle divination
system unlike anything ever published before.

Now you can easily explore and understand
the oracular and spiritual properties of
Ogham forest trees to new depths
and discover what lies beneath the mysteries
known only to the Oghamancers of old.

Beginners and adepts alike will find that
"The Book of Ogham"
is a handbook worth its weight in gold!

Joshua Free has been paving the way through
these woodland facets of nature magick for
over 25 years, and only now presents a
complete synthesis of his findings
– in print for the first time!

Once known only to the most elite members of
Celtic-Druid and Elven-Faerie traditions,
"The Book of Ogham" reveals hundreds of
associations and attributes concealing an entire
codified system of hidden cosmic wisdom.

If you want the best guide possible as your
companion in the folds of the magical forests,
then let "The Book of Ogham" by Joshua Free
be your map through the deep spiritual terrain
and mystic foliage of Celtic Tree Mysteries.

Titles in the forthcoming
2023 pocket paperback series
based on the *"Elvenomicon"*
written by Joshua Free

Coming soon from
JFI Publications

<u>Elvenomicon Series-I</u>

The Secret Book of Elven-Faerie

The Elven-Faerie Grimoire
The Enchanted Forest

<u>Elvenomicon Series-II</u>

Secret Legacy of Elves & Faeries
The Elven-Faerie Spellbook
The Book of Ogham

TABLET OF CONTENTS

INTRODUCTION

by Joshua Free

Research for *The Book of Ogham* began in the 1990's amidst a critical resurgence of 'New Age' revival—foremost among them regarding the *Celts* and *Druids*. *Book of Ogham* is an integral part of a greater body of work pertaining to my personal involvement with <u>*Pheryllt*</u> and <u>*Elven-Faerie*</u> traditions of Druidism for over 25 years. Both traditions were imparted to me directly by first-hand personal 'apprenticeships' with their modern developers in the mid-1990's. This is what is actually represented with my <u>*Draconomicon*</u> and <u>*Elvenomicon*</u> books, respectively to each.

The original "*Elvenomicon*" series—a trilogy —circulated underground as "*Book of Elven-Faerie*" but which I later renamed as *Elvenomicon* to avoid confusing the total collection of work with the title of the first discourse it contained: *Book of Elven-Faerie.* It is a separate volume from the other two parts in the trilogy: *The Elven-Faerie Grimoire* and *Enchanted Forest Grimoire.* Collectively this trilogy comprises *Elvenomicon* 'Series-1' and the first anthology of Elven-Faerie Druidry.

'Celtic Tree Mysteries' occupy intellectual and spiritual attention of all serious Druids or practitioners of the Elven-Faerie magical traditions. As one who continues to be enamored by the enchanting relationship that is maintained between Druid and 'Nature', the work toward codifying and systematizing Oghamic lore has been ongoing now for over a quarter-of-a-century, never seeming complete enough for a release into 'static' book form. It represents 'living knowledge' of the Earth that is constantly evolving. As such, although mentioned in no less than six of my previous publications, I have not presented a definitive *Book of Ogham* before.

The Book of Ogham picks up where *Greenwood Forest Grimoire* ('*The Enchanted Forest*') leaves off in the first *Elvenomicon* series/anthology. Over the years, many have asked me why 'such-and-such' wasn't included in the tree correspondences for that series. My answer remains that the first *Elvenomicon* series did not so much reflect my personal opinion or research as it did the preservation of a very specific 'Elven-Faerie' Druidic tradition and the lore representing it. Therefore, I did not unnecessarily alter what I was given.

One might also note that my former *Green-wood Forest Grimoire* (*'The Enchanted Forest'*) —in the first *Elvenomicon* series—focused on the 'trees' themselves; not necessarily the Ogham. *The Book of Ogham* examines oracular and spiritual lore of Oghamic tradition, whereas the former text emphasized physical tree properties and 'magical' lore.

It becomes apparent to a seasoned, well-acquainted, Seeker, that this new *Elvenomicon* series bridges 'Elven-Faerie' tradition with my 'Pheryllt Researches' and other various critical 'New Age' systems that have come (and often gone) during the past few decades leaving their footprints behind. These remind us of their own ventures to uncover secrets of the Great Mystery Tradition.

Many of the key literary contributions used as supportive research for this volume and published a mere thirty years ago (or less) are no longer even still "in print"—leaving only watered-down half-measure efforts of newer metaphysical authors in their place. Needless to say the pile of printed materials used to cross-reference *The Book of Ogham* research stacked up nearly as tall as I am.

After more than three decades of Celtic and Druidic revival efforts, we have now, at our disposal, a completely systematized Oghamic 'New Age' tradition of "divination" and "magic" to a degree that may or may not be one-to-one with its archaic presentation or usage, but which evolved into a fully workable system for modern purposes.

The Book of Ogham offers a Seeker the most complete correspondence lists and comprehensive divination symbolism of any single source ever published regarding Ogham. It also shines light on relationships between Ogham and other forms of divination—such as Tarot and the Nordic Runes—in order to gain greatest insight into the Ogham oracle as it evolved in various New Age traditions.

It is daunting to standardize what is otherwise an intuitive experiential pursuit by individual Druids. But, the Ogham is long due for a concise standard accessible to all practitioners of 'forest magick' and others in pursuit of 'Celtic Tree Mysteries'. May you find a clear map for your journey here.

—Joshua Free, Spring Equinox 2023
Borsippa HQ, San Luis Valley

THE
OGHAM

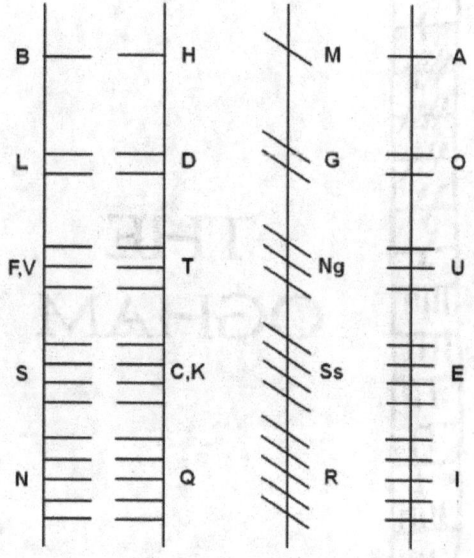

The traditional Ogham scale.

a brief history of the oghamic system

*"Ogma, a man well skilled in speech and in poetry,
invented the Ogham. The cause of its invention,
as proof of his ingenuity, and that this speech
should belong to the learned exclusively.
The father of Ogham is Ogma. The mother of
Ogham is the hand or knife of Ogma."*

—'Lebor Ogaim'

Ogham or 'Ogam' (properly pronounced as 'ow-am' 'oh-wam' 'oh-am' 'ohm' according to various sources) is a style of script—and, of course, 'sigils', 'glyphs' or 'runes' in New Age applications. It represents information once unique to upper classes of Celtic society—particularly the *Druids*, who in fact decreed it forbidden for the uninitiated to be given practical knowledge of the alphabet.

The surviving literary records of scholarly and mystical interest today are notably Irish (Gaelic) manuscripts and various esoteric British (usually Welsh) sources—all of which have been considered during preparation of this present handbook.

Ancient Celtic and Druid Ogham inscriptions do still survive today on hundreds of 'standing stones' and 'markers' in Ireland and the British Isles. Many more likely exist but are badly damaged. Notches or hash-marks (called '*fleasc*' or '*fleasg*') distinguishing each letter or "*few*" ('*fidh*'—or "*fews*"/ '*fedha*' plural) are written along a straight-edge—or the "*stemline*" ('*droim*'). Of course, when cut onto stone, the outer edges are most vulnerable to wear.

"Stemline" (the straight-line) / "*droim*"
"Notch" (hash-marks) / "*fleasc*"
"*Few*" (an individual letter) / "*fidh*"
"*Fews*" (letters, plural) / "*fedha*"

Ancient wooden Ogham artifacts rarely survived the ages. The best examples date only to the 1700's and relate to an entirely separate Celtic alphabet—the Bardic *coelbren*—used almost exclusively in the Welsh-Druid tradition and based on researches of Iolo Morganwg in Wales. But the secret alphabet of Ogham was not always intended for obvious permanence or detection. For example, wooden posts or temporary signs could be raised near remote settlements or villages that might alert a traveling Druid to secret grove meetings and perhaps inform of their location. To the uninitiated, such ambiguous notches would not seem significant.

Not surprisingly, origins of the Ogham are frequently attributed to Ireland—where a host of manuscripts and majority of surviving 'sites' remain. As with many of the other archetypes and stereotypes of "Celtic" culture, Ireland served as the last great stronghold for Celtic and Druidic tradition —meaning the most recently in our history.

Prior to this, the Celtic and Druidic influence dominated most of ancient Europe up until the 'Classical period' (the age of Romans and Greeks) when Celtic-Druid presence was forced westward—primarily due to ancient 'Romanticization' and later, the eventual 'Christianization' of Europe. Thus, as it is an alphabet, not a dialect, most surviving Ogham inscriptions represent the Irish language in Ireland.

The secret alphabet notably emerged into use during a time when hidden messages might need to be exchanged among Druids amidst interaction with a literate classical world of Greeks and Romans. It is difficult to determine the origins definitively, even archaeologically, because Ogham script was never intended for widespread open visibility or any common use among the Celts. But there is a surge of more visible usage in the Celtic world *c.* 100 BC.

According to the Irish texts, Ogham script originated (or was refined) *c.* 600-500 BC. by the scribe-poet-god of the Celtic pantheon: Oghma—named Ogma, Ogmios or Ogmas in other Celtic/Druidic traditions. In addition to gifting Druidism with knowledge of the Ogham script, he became something of a 'patron deity' in the Bardic tradition.

Oghma is listed as one of the "Tuatha de Danaan" (or "Tuatha d'Anu" in the original *Elvenomicon* series), or else the Danubian Druids that arrived in Ireland when it was formerly occupied by the "Fir Bolg" and "Formorian" races. As such, he is related to Dagda and Lugh (also famous Celtic deities).

Although dating on the findings are often disputed, chalk slabs once excavated by Alexander Keiller in southern England (Windmill Hill, Avebury, Wiltshire) suggest that ancient prehistoric Oghamic use may have existed there as early as 2160 B.C. concurrent with a dawning 'Age of Aries' and the development of Mardukite Babylon.

The era of the historical Oghma is the same time, archaeologically speaking, that the 'La Tene' type of Celts are believed to have emerged prominently in Ireland—after migrated westward across Europe. This era is marked not only by increasing contact between Celts and the classical world, but also an internal Celtic integration of proto-Druidic, proto-Celtic and La Tene cultures.

THE OGHAM TREE ALPHABET

An Oghamic (or proto-Oghamic) tradition appears to be related to at least some methods employed to preserve Druid lore in ancient times. While historians are inclined to suggest that Celtic society was wholly illiterate, there is strong evidence to support the existence of ancient Druid 'tree libraries' in remote forests. Leaves, representing information, were hung on strings or 'stemlines', much like the 'written' or 'inscribed' Ogham script later represents.

The Romans reportedly destroyed hundreds of these forest libraries during their efforts to conquer the Celtic people—an effort that lasted for half of a millennium.

Modern Ogham lore is drawn from surviving manuscripts of antiquity, some dating back as far as the Medieval times, in the heart of the Dark Ages; most of which are, in fact, Irish—including *Book of Ballymote* and *Lebor Ogaim* (*The Book of Ogham*, also known as the *Ogham Tract*) and *The Scholar's Primer* among others. But it should be understood that these are archaic works *about* the Ogham; we have no surviving manuscripts actually written *in* Ogham.

The alphabet is structured into four groups of five *fews*; each group is called an *aicme*. Much like Nordic runes, it can actually be utilized to write in most any language. It is read left-to-right when the *stemline* is horizontal (meaning the right side of an upright *few* faces down), or it is read upward when inscribed vertically—an orientation point.

Although primarily used as a 'secret code' and alphabet among the elite, the scholarly and 'Druidic' applications included 'coded'

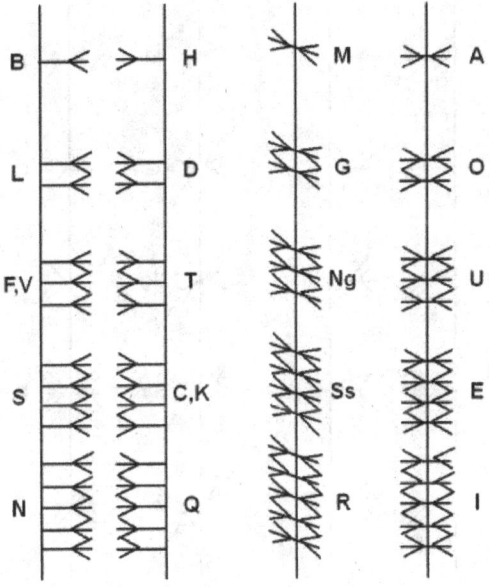

Ogham scale variation from Book of Ballymote.

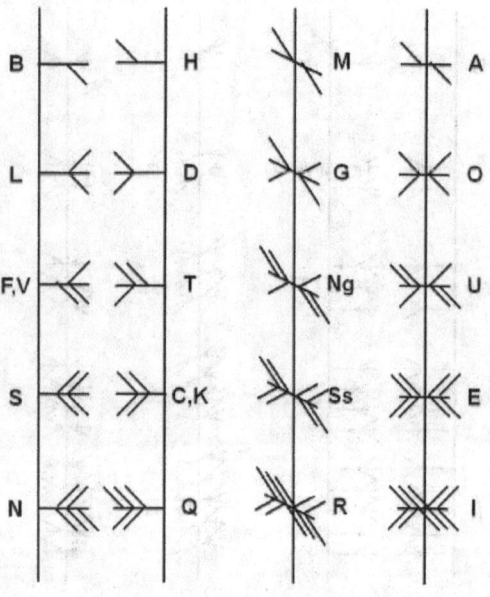

Ogham scale variation from Book of Ballymote.

references to all manners of birds, animals, stones, deities, places, and above all else for our interests: the names of *trees*. In fact, the Oghamic tradition concealed a mnemonic code used to assist recall of vast systematized knowledge lessons in Druidic tradition.

Archaic manuscripts suggest that as many as 150 different "Oghams" may have been memorized by the Ovates and Bards of the Druid College—"Tree Ogham" being only one of them, but obviously one that became most popular for modern 'New Age' metaphysical and/or magical (magickal) purposes. There are also nearly 100 variations (or "scales") of Ogham script given in the *Book of Ballymote* alone. Two are shown here.

Throughout the world of magic and mysticism, across aeons of folklore and mythology, trees have stood as the universal or cosmic symbol of the connection between all 'worlds' or "Universes"—referred to in esoteric lore as the "World Tree" or axis link between *this* physical-material Universe or level of perception (referred to as "a beta-existence" in Systemology) and the true all-encompassing "Other" existence.

The theme appears in other esoteric models as the "Tree of Life"—such as in the "Kabbalah" of the Ancient Near East, &tc. Apart from the "Dragon," the "Tree" is the most commonly reoccurring ancient cosmological model of all Universes and Creation.

It is not surprising then that we should find evidence of both the 'Dragon' and the 'Tree' as definitive icons of Druidic Tradition. In the Celtic cosmology, the physical universe is likened to a "dragon" and the "tree" represents the conduit that connects *this* "Mid-Branch" (or "Middle-Earth") existence with *upper* and *lower* existences. Ancient Mesopotamians maintained similar lore in their mythological symbolism of existence. But, let us turn our attention more concisely to the Ogham itself...

[The following transcript is a special bonus for this edition that would not have been available for inclusion a few years ago.]

MARDUKITE MASTER COURSE ACADEMY LECTURE #22[*]

"the oghamic tradition"

One of the features of *Merlyn's Complete Book of Druidism*—as a Master Course edition for present purposes that wasn't available when we released previous editions of the past, like, as an anthology (*The Druid Compleat*)—but this edition has the complete notebooks of my "*Pheryllt Researches*" and portions of the *Pheryllt Researches* were then spliced with excerpts that went along with those themes, when I composed "*Book of Pheryllt: A Complete Druid Source Book*," originally published by 'Kima Global' to go along with "*Deepteachings of Merlyn*" and Douglas Monroe's complete "*Merlyn Trilogy*."[‡]

---

[*] Transcript of a lecture given by Joshua Free on September 24, 2020; extracted from "*Druids, Elves & Dragons: Mardukite Master Course Academy Lectures (Volume II)*"—also contained in "*The Complete Mardukite Master Course*."

[‡] Now available in a collector's edition hardcover from JFI Publishing as "*Draconomicon Vol. 2: The Pheryllt Researches*" and within the new

So, what I did in this edition is I maintained the material that is in *Elvenomicon* presently still today as it's been for the last fifteen years, and then added as an appendix to the entire book, the "*Pheryllt Researches*." And so, if you are going to deal with Master-level 'Ogham Tech' or forest magick and a "Druid School," this is some pretty critical stuff to incorporate.

I expect in the next couple years—I've been asked to expand on my work on the "Elven-Faerie Tradition" and "Druidism" and many other elements of Grade-I. Rowen Gardner contributed some 'Forewords' to, I believe, the *Druid's Handbook* and the *Draconomicon* in the past. I've done some work with them in the past. So, I decided to go ahead and probably work with them on expanding Grade-I material—for those that are using it, again, as an entry-point; and for those who are still coming into our tradition.

So... *expect that* to be coming up here; but what I do want to do is present—a lot of the material is already present within the Mast-

_____

2023 deluxe anthology, "*The Complete Book of Pheryllt: Lost Secrets of the Druids*."

er Course, it's just not set up that way. So, again, if you look through the material and the "Instructor's Manual" and look at the material of the *Pheryllt Researches* in addition to *Elvenomicon* and the *Draconomicon*, *Druid's Handbook*, you'll see that this time around already, the "Route of Druidism and Dragon Legacy" exceeds anything we were presenting as *"The Druid Compleat"* in the past.

At a Grade-I understanding, you will find a lot of material as you go into the *"Greenwood Grimoire"* of the *Elvenomicon*—or even the *Vampyre's Handbook*—you're going to see more of an emphasis on work with "Rays of Light," which is really just getting someone into a practice of handling "flows."

Handling "energy flows" directly is actually a very high level element of "Alpha" work— of Wizard work. It's practiced at Grade-I levels; but seldom mastered. Because when we're dealing with "Rays of Light," when we're dealing with the "flows," the channels between individuals, the "conduits," a lot of this... and the way it's explained in the *Vampyre's Handbook*, it's all handling, basically, raw energy directly.

Now, we've found as an alternative to this, that handling "mental imagery"—or even the concepts of which these various "flows" and "energies" and response-mechanisms are attached—is actually a lot more effective; a lot easier. There's nothing wrong with handling the "energies" directly. It's just that at a Grade-I level, when an individual is usually just now getting used to the concept that these even exist, it's usually considered higher-level work within even that grade, to start handling "Rays" and such directly.

The other element being: astral light—the concept of an "astral body." We know now at kind of a higher systemological level that these 'astral bodies' are kind of "blanketing" this existence that we have here; they're basically bodies that have actually almost—not deteriorated—but they no longer have the same "power" and "function" and "solidity" to occupy as a point-of-view as, for example, what we're kind of stuck in *here*.

And that's why we're trying to liberate an individual *out of* the Human Condition while we're doing Systemology work. These "astral bodies" do perhaps occupy a "mental plane"

—"mental universes"—once operating very much as a "beta-existence" within themselves, but for whatever reasons enough barriers, blockages, withholding—in terms of wanting to reach, and withdrawing *from*— and other elements forced more and more condensed point-of-views of what we experience today as *reality*.

"Astral work"—"mental work"—*can* be employed; it's just that we have found at higher levels of practice that there are simply more effective ways (than what is demonstrated in conventional mysticism). I mention this because the concept of the "Astral Grove" is introduced within my writings—within the last fifteen years—mostly ever since I kinda came to the realization that there was a way to get back to this other "Magical Universe" that we've all descended from. One of the ways in which I thought practice of that could be involved, was getting back to the point where *Self* was able to experience... well...

There's a reason why those that are attached —or find an attraction to—have any affinity with "Druidic Paths," the "Elven Paths," the "Faerie Paths," things that involve "Nature,"

"Shamanism," animals and so forth; there's a reason why there's an inclination: because this restimulates a memory—probably several lifetimes worth of memory—involving this other Universe, this other existence, which one did engage in a very fluid communication and perfect understanding with what was treated *there* as the "natural world."

There is a "mirror image" of it on *our* planet, although not nearly as vibrant until you're actually able to peel away some of these "levels" of (fragmentation) that kind of dim our sight of this world. But there's a connection there because it does "remind" us exactly of that; and that when we looked at, for example in yesterday's lectures, some of the traditions and Faerie traditions and Otherworld beliefs concerning this existence and whatever existence that these once physical and inhabiting "elves" and so forth—"Faerie Races"—that inhabited this physical existence and we able to be identified as such, were then moving *back* to the "Magical Universe" and taking up residence there.

Now, what we've later discovered was that this Universe became kind of a lower-level

consideration or "prison" or "penalty existence" of a lower-level Game than what was
taking place in the "Magical Universe." At
that level of existence, we had the original
archetypes of what you see with "Wizardry"
and "mysticism" and "magic" and the natural "elements" and related icons and themes
that draw someone into this tradition.

As one of the "Masters" or the "Instructors"
involved with the Mardukite Academy, you
would then be able to recognize these elements and work with them later on in "processing"—if you get into "Piloting" or other
elements and the higher "Wizard levels." Because these are direct links. These are what's
going to get individuals out of the confines
of the Human Condition.

Many that are taking up these paths already
have some kind of inkling that there *is* something more and that they're not strictly "Human" as *Self*. I mean, these are all things that
many carry with them today. Just because
they're not involved with *us*, doesn't mean
they aren't aware of these things. But...*selective directed attention!* That's what we've
emphasized in Systemology; and most indiv-

iduals that aren't carrying a *full* realization of what's taking place, it's overshadowed by all the other aspects of the material world.

In terms of "Elven Tradition," "Celtic Faerie Tradition," "tree magic," "forest magick"— there are ceremonies for the "Consecration of a Newly Planted Tree," a "Rite for Planting a Single Guardian Tree" and "Dedications of a Grove" or "Stewardship of an Area" are all within what was originally called the *Greenwood Forest Grimoire* in the *Elvenomicon*, which appears in *Merlyn's Complete Book of Druidism*.

One of the reasons I had at one point encouraged more "Astral Grove" work was because the "Elven Fellowship Circle of Magick" was meeting in Denver. Most of the work I did on the *Elvenomicon*, up until 2004, was while living in Denver. Although there were a lot of parks and, of course, access to the mountains and Nature, I was writing, primarily at the time, for what is considered "urban" readership; and so the concept of using an "Astral Grove" or using "imaginative creative visualization" to operate "magick" was simply as an alternative to, you know, access to "natural terrain" or natural areas to operate.

So, if an individual wasn't able to physically actually go to a park or go to an area or have a "grove" to work from or maintain stewardship of or guardianship of, then using the "Astral Grove"—using visualization techniques—was an alternative. And this is something I still do impress as a very effective form of "magick" that virtually any of the results that can be achieved from actually working out a ritual area, drawing out a physical space, using physical tools, physical implements an all that—can actually be practiced *within* the "mental realm" because that's actually all you're trying to achieve anyways.

The *Self* is using the "body" and the fact it's kind of been restricted to this point-of-view of a "body" at still this point of Grade-I, that is has to basically get the body—what we like to do in "objective processing" in Systemology—we're command of the body involved, and more command and control of the Mind-System that's doing that, by doing these outward "objective universe" practices.

If the same states can be achieved in the Mind without that—if an individual is able to achieve that—then all of this can actually be done at that level directly; in simply the operation of the Mind-System. Of course, this doesn't replace what we're trying to impress with the "Natural Paths" and "Ogham Tech" and actually going out into Nature and engaging into these lessons directly. But again, this is one of the elements that's not necessarily relayed in the "ritual magick" texts or in what's considered "mainstream New Age mysticism"—that all of these are meant to be tools, meant to assist the individual Seeker, into achieving this greater control over the Mind-Body connection or control over the Mind-System or actually Actualizing Self as a Spiritual Being as the Alpha-Spirit.

That's what we're dealing with all the way up the *Pathway*. But like we've said before: sometimes a passive—or just a simple read-through—or basic demonstration into what we consider a Grade-I understanding of the "New Age" or "Magick and Mysticism" is not a guarantee that an individual is going to surpass that and reach to new levels of realization; especially if they're tied exclusively to a "magickal correspondence in the physical universe" type of understanding.

OGHAM TECH.

But in terms of these assistant tools—within Ogham Tech, we have Ogham Sticks: they're twenty sticks or twigs, same size, cut the same size, polished; I mentioned before you could use "wood chips" if you wanna make more "rune stone" styles. But these are specifically for divination and cryptomancy— and so each of them, you would have twenty, and each of them would have one of the standard Ogham "*fews*" or characters; either carved into, or if possible, burned onto.

And then Ogham Wands are a completely different set of tools. These can range from six to eighteen inches. And if possible, what you want to do is construct them from the correlating trees. Thus, you have a "hazel wand" that's taken from the "hazel tree" and so forth.

If you look into the *Elvenomicon*—in the back, where we deal a lot with the tree lore—you'll see that there's a lot of correspondences and other ways of connecting attributes of tree energies so that you can find substitute trees that could represent the same kind of energy pattern. And so each one of them, what you want to do is you have a long rod and then this kind of section up at the top that you have as like a handle, you kinda cut away this to shave it flat so that it kinda goes down into the middle and this kinda gives you this surface to either burn or paint one of the Ogham "fews" on.

Traditionally these are used specifically for "tree communication" and communing with Nature. So these wands we kinda sharpen the other point a bit, you know, cut it down to a point. And this is then put into the ground and so the individual, when their communing with a specific energy or their working on a specific "Path of Encounter" or what have you, they have this Wand into the ground and then they're holding the handle part here where the Ogham script is printed.

That's what these particular ones are for—and since their each used individually and their not "cast" as any kind of divination, you don't need to be too concerned with, you know, making them all the same size or anything of that nature. Each is an individual tool.

And then there's the Ogham Rods. Twenty-one pieces of the same size, like, dowels. You just cut dowels down into twenty-one little sticks that are all the same size, and you don't do anything to them. They're basically just "cast" out as, kind of like, the game of "*pick up sticks*"—they're just "cast" out and you "read" any... however they've fallen, you "read" any of the Ogham symbols or script patterns in there that you might then look up to interpret as some sort of "omen."

Traditionally they've referred to the "magic pouch" that an "Oghamancer" or a "forest wizard" would use, as the "Crane Bag"—because the crane is the animal of knowledge. When it would fly in the air—its legs and the way it would stand and different patterns it would make—they would interpret those as Ogham symbols as well. So they had these *bags* that are called "Crane Bags." And each of your sets—your Ogham Sticks and Rods—they could each have their own Crane Bag.

The Wands, you can kind of arrange those. I've—when I've done this in the past, I had my own little wooden chest that I made; and I just kept all the various lengths of wood in there that way. So those are several tools that you can use; and you can correlate—you know, throughout this material, there's all kinds of Ogham correspondences and correlations... ways of practicing divination and interpreting Earth mysteries; these are basically the tools you might use for that.

I should point out: although I don't really recommend the printed card medium for this, the original presentation, or the reintroduction actually of this lore, the idea of a "Celtic Tree Oracle" for the New Age, really is attributed Liz and Colin Murray, which in 1988 released the "*Celtic Tree Oracle*" with St. Martin's Press. It's this beautiful green hardcover book and these cards. This has been basically the inspiration for much of the modern neopagan and "New Age" Celtic Tree lore connected to the Ogham in the past few decades. This inspired interest in the Ogham, when prior to that, it was more of an academic or scholarly interest regarding Ogham inscriptions found on stones all throughout Celtic Britain and Ireland. There's actually even evidence that they existed in the mainland of Europe, and even the Americas.

And so this interest in using the "Celtic" Ogham to represent a system of "Celtic Tree Magic" sprung up from that. When mixed with thousands of years of tree lore it has since evolved into what's become an entire complete system and field of "magick." And there's many examples of... each tree listed in the back of the *Elvenomicon* or *Merlyn's Complete Book of Druidism*. *Pheryllt Researches* also include many correspondences and applications and just a wealth of material.*

TREE-ORACLE ELF-STONES.

One of the key tools also that I've kind of always popularized—I mean, I started this with the original *Sorcerer's Handbook*; it was given in the "Merlyn Stone" materials and also I've expanded it in terms of the *Elvenomicon* and have plans to take this (subject) further, as I said, when I expand my publications concerning Route-D type materials (which will be coming out in the next couple of years).

So, this concept of "Elfstones"—they weren't necessarily referred to as "Elfstones" in anci-

---

* Much of this is synthesized and expanded on in this present volume, *The Book of Ogham*.

ent Celtic lore. What I did was... —I was fascinated with the "Shannara" series of Terry Brooks; and perhaps as one of his better known, it became the subject of the "Season One" presentation of it a few years back when they did actually make a televised version of it. Fans had been hoping for a motion picture of his book "Elfstones of Shannara" for decades—and it was finally picked up essentially as a miniseries.

In the original concept of the Elfstones, there are three stones which had significance as a powerful tool; this set of stones. In that particular version, they were three blue stones. And I have this set that are three blue stones and what I use them for is "clarity of vision." They were considered "seeing stones" in one version of the stories by Terry Brooks, and so that's one way that I've used them. I've also used three green stones as a way of basically getting in touch with the "Green World" while working with the natural elements or "Middle Ray"—the "crystalline ray"—you know, things of that nature.

Traditional Elfstones that appear (in Celtic lore) are known as "sky stones" or "triscale stones." They've been popularized in some books of Celtic wisdom derived from mythologies; they've been found in—for example, the Pheryllt system in *21 Lessons of Merlyn.*

So, the traditional set is: a golden stone, a silver stone, and what would be a crystalline stone or a black stone. And these each represent: the "Golden Ray," the "Silver Ray" and "Crystal Ray" of the "Druid's Cabala"; and the "Ray" system of the "Rays of Light" as they pertain to, not only the "Elven" system, but any of the "Light-Center" systems or "Chakra" systems—any "Seven-Plus-One" systems that involve Lights, which we deal with all throughout the various grades.

And so these are actually a really good tool for getting in touch with basic divination and tree communication. They have kind of a "pendulum"—like a "yes-or-no" quality to them; and so when they're used, the crystalline stone or black stone is used as an indicator. The silver is used to indicate "no" and the gold indicates "yes." And when you throw them—or "cast" them—at the base of the Oracle Tree, whatever stone is closest to the indicator stone is your answer.

The traditional "set" consists of the Tiger's Eye for the golden stone, the Hematite for the silver stone and Obsidian for the black stone. And this, again, you can keep in a small pouch and keep separate; or if you want to make several steps the way I've... you know, a standard set that I've had since the 90's: the hematite, obsidian and tiger's eye. I also have (this) blue set and a green set and each I use for different purposes.

But these basic, just, focal tools—these basic implements... Again, it's not to put a lot of emphasis on the power that they themselves have, but over the significance that is attributed to it by using them—by using them as a focus or to concentrate on a particular "Ray" or particular state or particular aspect. And so for *that* purpose, they can be very useful; very useful tools for increasing sensitivity.

THE OGHAM LADDER OF LEARNING.

So, before closing this out, I *do* want to give a brief rundown of the actual Ogham trees—and the most applicable way to do this, for the purpose of our Master Course, is to look at it from the perspective of "The 21 Paths of

Encounter." You can look at the Ogham for their individual aspects—what they represent. Each Ogham represents a color, it represents a bird, it represents a particular magical lesson—it does also represent a tree. You can easily use all of these aspects in "ritual magic." You can also use all them for divinatory or oracular purposes.

But I thought, for the purposes of the Master Course, I would run through this "Druid's Cabala of the Forest" with you—and how it's presented in climbing the "Great Tree of Life" in the Oghamic tradition. The concept of "Ascending the Druid's Ladder" is interpreted from the Pheryllt tradition.

This is not in the "Master Course Instructor's Manual," but it is in our Master Edition textbook of "*Merlyn's Complete Book of Druidism*"— in the *Pheryllt Researches* section. And what this lore does is: this runs through the basic Ogham trees and the Ogham symbolism in the order in which it's given traditionally. And it's usually—they're in groups of five.

We start with the *Birch Tree*, which represents new beginnings, first realizations, self-sacrifice, change to a higher level, devotion to the Great Work, awakening on the path.

And then we move onto the *Rowan Tree*, the first action, the first move of a game, magical work begun, self-control, movement in the direction of your chosen path.

Then we go to the third path, *Alder*, which represents heated resistance, strength to face what's avoided, conquering adversaries, the material world opposes your choice but your aspirations are completely protected.

The fourth path is *Willow*: new journeys and inspiration, Otherworld contact, confidence necessary, enchantment. Your path now appears as a dream on a moonlit night.

The fifth path: *Ash*; personal resolve, resolute decision, changing outlooks, the inner and outer world meet as one, and the inertia to break the threshold. And by threshold, we mean approaching the veil—the first veil of threshold—which is the "death of the old."

So, we've ascended up the path to the sixth Ogham now, *Hawthorn*—where new blossoms awaken. This represents the first success or manifestation being purified, protection given as you accept the bitter and the sweet of the chosen Path. And the bitter and the sweet is interesting, because in the upper level, when we're talking about flows and concepts in upper-level processing, we're actually talking about the "beauty" and the "ugliness," the light and the dark, the compelling versus the repulsion and all of that. This is something that actually as you break through the "Death of the Old," this is actually what we're trying to *flatten* out; *flatten* out any reactivity to.

The seventh path, the *Oak*: higher powers experienced and called to you, the strong door to the inner mysteries. Oak is spoken "*duir*" in Celtic languages. This is where we get the word "*Door*"—and then, of course, the "*Oaken Door*" is a strong common use for the wood, traditionally. Personal reflection opens up to new possibilities; we're talking about opening up "doors" to inner mysteries.

Which leads us to the eighth path, *Holly*. This represents an encounter, the Guardian of the Gates—which of course, we're approaching this Door; this Gateway—self-worth is tested, balance of opposition, challenge is presented, things may not always be what they seem so dispel all illusion.

And then we work into *Hazel*. Hazel is the ninth path: the fruit of knowledge. As we know, hazelnut—this kinda goes with other traditions from Druidry—the hazelnut falls into the lake, which is then eaten by the salmon, and then the bear eats the salmon. And these all become animals and trees and symbols of "knowledge"—of ancient knowledge and paths of knowledge and ancient primordial wisdom. So, from the hazel, the fruit of knowledge is given, wisdom is accessible, your encounter yields straightforward harvest of secret intuitions.

The tenth path: *Apple*—the tree of beauty. So, we have this new enchantment that comes with breaking through this first veil—the enchantment—such as like the *lunar level* with these new realizations and awakening these prior purposes and feeling the enchantment of Otherworld contact. This brings us to the second veil or threshold, which is that "Matter Gives Way to Mystery." And so we're confronting "Mystery"—*flattening the* Mystery—eliminating "Mystery" now.

And the eleventh path is the *Vine*, which is a meeting of companions, fellowship is born and hidden knowledge is revealed between them, strength to face destinies, your path is entangled with... fate, prophecy of others.

The twelfth path: *Ivy*. And Ivy, of course, is the "spiral"—the "spiral" of the Path—when you look at the growth patterns of Ivy; overcoming restrictions—Ivy, of course, breaking through barriers to be able to continue its growth, gaining confidence, inner strength and continuing to face the world; confront.

And the thirteenth path is *Blackthorn*: facing material existence, the clutches of the world, transition and change along the path, death, loss, cleansing, clearing; when choices are taken away, the perfect path remains. And there you see another staple of the *Pathway to Self-Honesty*.

The fourteenth path: *Reed*. Experience in the world; learning from experience, understanding Earth systems, material struggle, survival, knowing selective conform; knowing when to bend.

The *Elder*: self-annihilation; purging the Self

of all artificial, the darkness before dawn; the "Dark Night of the Soul" so to speak; facing hard truths, accepting the lessons given and seeing clear light ahead.

Which brings us to the last set—the Third Veil—which is "Visions of Victory." And here we're coming down the "Home Path" here. It begins with the *Fir* or *Pine tree* of high views, long sight, the depth of relationships; experience gives rise to new visions and new realizations; seeing past the illusions—and even getting past our own experiences—the distant clear path that is visible.

The seventeenth path, *Furze*: the sweet smell of victory; awareness of the seeds born of difficulty; struggle passes away; and there's time to rest as you collect yourself. Here's where you're basically reaching that *point* where you're—it's either going to be a divide and conquer or conquest versus succumb.

And so at this point, you also have the eighteenth path: *Heather*. Pause and reflection; healing of the spirit; examination of actions —we're talking about hostile acts and withholds, withholding from others and withholding from ourselves; we're talking about the responsibility, taking responsibility and Self-determination; we're talking about basically making one's Self "whole" so that one can aspire to the remainder of the journey.

Which, in the nineteenth path, *Aspen*: you have the rainbow kaleidoscope of spiritual achievement appearing before you; protection given on the "Rainbow Path"—you see many references here to the "horizons of many colors" and a "Rainbow Path." It's also —this is applicable to the Tower of Babel, and the "Tower" of the Tarot; and so we're talking directly here of a "Ladder of Lights" —Ascension—the 'Ascent' up the "Ladder of Lights" beyond what has been... Breaking the gravity of the material existence.

The twentieth path, *Yew*, is: completion, final realizations, Ascension, rising above the impermanent, the product of the journey—the end in the beginning; beginning in the end.

Finally, twenty-first path, *Mistletoe*, represents the "formless," the "not," the "unknowable." We're talking about the Infinite. So we have the twenty-first element representing "Infinity of Nothingness," which we know is, the true background beyond the ALL.

THE
TREES

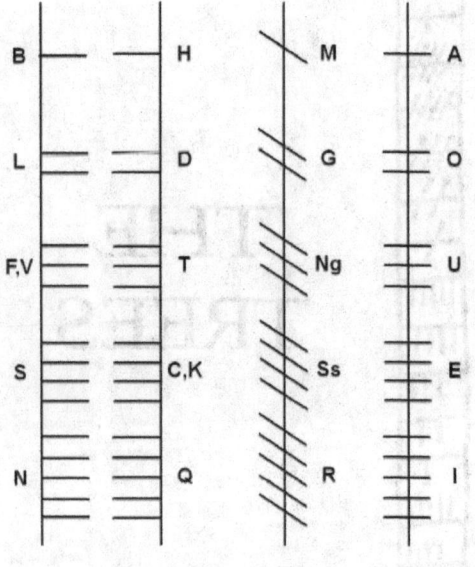

OGHAM FEWS DESCRIPTION KEY

"Standard Names (Celtic and English)."
"Esoteric Text Quote"
[Background Information]

ESOTERIC CORRESPONDENCE.

Alternate Names : Variations of spelling
demonstrated by various Celtic
languages (*Irish, Welsh, &tc*).

Alphabet Letter : Standard character.

Ogma's Tree : An associated tree of "Ogma
Sun-Face" recorded in the Irish
"*Lebor Ogaim*" ('*The Ogham Tract*').

Alternate Trees : Other species with similar
energetic/spiritual properties.

Bardic Value : Numeric designation based
on traditional Ogham sequential
arrangement; also any reductions
using *classical numerology*; the term
"Bardic Value" was popularized by
Colin (and Liz) Murray's Ogham
work for "*The Celtic Tree Oracle*."

Forest Rank (British) : Using the hierarchy of
the forest listed in the *Ogham Forest*

Tract of British Druids—*chieftain, peasant, shrub* or *bramble*.

Forest Rank (Irish) : As above for Irish Druids.

Quadratic Element : Corresponding 'classical element'—*earth, air, fire* or *water*.

Druid Guardian : Name given from the *'Boibel-Loth'* Ogham; used similarly in practice as 'patron saints'.

Celtic Deities : Avatars/heroes of the Celtic Mythos that identify with similar energetic/spiritual qualities.

Druidic Deities : Figures of Celtic Religion given on a mnemonic list (from at least the 1st Century B.C.) that is related to the Ogham alphabet.

Solar Month : A standard calendar month as adopted from Elven-Faerie Druidry (given in the *Elvenomicon*); there is *no* universal esoteric standard for a 'Celtic Tree Calendar'.

Lunar Month : A month of the pagan/lunar 'Wheel of the Year' or one of the 'Sabbats' (Grove Festivals); often based on the work of Robert Graves; lunar months are traditionally indicated by Full Moons starting

with one closest to the 'Winter
Solstice' (or Samhain as 'New Year')
—however, there is *no* consistent
Ogham calendar among sources.

Color Ogham : As recorded in the Irish "*Lebor
Ogaim*" (*Ogham Tract*).

Bird Ogham : As recorded in the Irish "*Lebor
Ogaim*" (*Ogham Tract*).

Sacred Animal : As given in various *Ogham
Tracts* and 'New Age' sources, &tc.

Sacred Gems : Corresponding 'gemstones'
with a similar energetic/spiritual
quality, as adopted from Elven-
Faerie Druidry lore and other 'New
Age' sources.

Ogham Forest Tract : Additional practical,
oracular and/or energetic/spiritual
expressions associated; keywords
collected from *Tracts*, the *Scholar's
Primer* and other records; an associated "art" or "craft" is also given.

DIVINATION SYMBOLISM.

Description : A written description of the
graphic/glyph or '*few*' character.

Word Ogham (Morann mac Main) : Given in
Auraicept na n'Eces (*Scholars Primer*);
alternate name, Morainn mac Moin.

Word Ogham (Mac Ind Oic) : As recorded in
Auraicept na n'Eces (*Scholars Primer*);
alternately, 'Ogham of Aonghus'.

Tarot Equivalent : For divinatory purposes—
a traditional Tarot Key (card) from
the standard Major Arcana that
represents this Ogham *few*.

Ogham Lochlannach : Corresponding (Norse)
Runic Key interpreted similarly as
given in *Ogham Tracts* of Ballymote.

Personality : When used to indicate specific
persons, known or unknown, this
Key may be consulted (as similar
to use of "court" cards in Tarot);
an 'inverted' trait is also included.

Oracular Meaning : A list of representative
factors, states or aspects traditionally interpreted for each Ogham
Key—derived from Celtic-Druid
and/or Elven-Faerie lore; concepts/
attributes may also be attracted by
"ritual" or "meditation"; or for use
as symbolism for talismans, &tc.

1. *beith* — **birch tree**

"The birch tree reminds us that new dimensions are opening for us. As they do, balance is necessary for greatest success in entering them."

—Ted Andrews
'Nature-Speak'

In the starting position of Ogham script, the birch tree signifies initiation and inception of a new journey or endeavor. A youthful vitality is infused in these new undertakings that is not reliant on experience. In fact, the birch is indicative of a need to release a hold on the past, clearing out old energies and taking up a path of spiritual Self-cleansing—or else the pathway of personal 'defragmentation'.

ESOTERIC CORRESPONDENCE.

Alternate Names : beithe, beth, belwen, beath

Alphabet Letter : "B"

Ogma's Tree : "birch in the forest"

Alternate Trees : beech (*phagos*), river-birch

Bardic Value : 1 (unity and purity); also the singularity or source, union of all forces/energies in rawest form

Alternative (R.Graves) : 5

Forest Rank (British) : Chieftain

Forest Rank (Irish) : Peasant

Quadratic Element : Air

Druid Guardian : Boibel ('Babel')

Celtic Deities : Bel, Mabon; also Amergin
(creativity), Blodeuwedd (learning
lessons), Credne (creativity), Deae
Matres (children), Evnissyen
(responsibility), Finvarra (comp-
etition), Grannos (purification),
O'Carolan (creativity)

Druidic Deities : Bran (the 'Raven', protection, power), Belinos (sun god of
fire, healing, inspiration) Barinthus
(the 'Ferryman', teaching, mystery)

Solar Month : November 1 ("New Year");
the day after *Samhain*, start of the
first month

Lunar Month : December 24 – January 20/21;
begins closest to Winter Solstice;
Moon of Inception; Moon of Beginnings (uses 'Yule' as the 'New Year'
or start of the first month); some
esoteric discrepancy on whether a

'New' or 'Full' moon denotes the
start of a 'lunar month'

Color Ogham : *ban*, white

Bird Ogham : *besan*, pheasant

Sacred Animal : cow (goddess, nurturing)

Sacred Gems : flourite, red-sard, imperial
topaz

Ogham Forest Tract : wands, broomsticks,
protection (wards) for children,
healing, greatness, eagerness

Arts of Civilization : *bethumnacht*, livelihood

DIVINATION SYMBOLISM.

Description : one notch to the right of the
stemline (or downward facing if a
horizontal stemline)

Word Ogham (Morann mac Main) : "*Feocus
foltchain*—faded trunk and fair hair"

Word Ogham (Mac Ind Oic) : "*Glaisiuni cnis*—
most silvery of skin"

Tarot Equivalent : The Star—future accomp-
lishments, high hopes and ideals,
need for clarity and spiritual aid

Ogham Lochlannach : *jera*—fertility, harvest,

peace; also 'year' or 'good year', alteration, transformation, turning, revolution of circumstance, fulfillment of plans; but also inversion, sudden setbacks, reversals; a major change; (also *berkana* rune or 'birch tree', beginnings, birth, &tc,)

Personality : happy
  Inversion : immature

Oracular Meaning : new beginnings (a new start at a higher level), renewal (revitalized energy), cleansing, purification, fertility, new birth (or rebirth), vitality, new dedication to the Pathway (the 'Great Work'), the 'Lady of the Woods'

2. *luis* — **rowan tree**

"Seek ever the way of the soul,
whereby or by what order, having served the body
to the same order to which it did flow
that it may rise up again,
joining action to sacred speech."

—Oracle of the Mystic Rowan
(Monroe Version)

The rowan tree indicates the first challenges faced after setting upon the Pathway—but the Seeker is well prepared to face (or confront) these directly, and is well-protected via new insights recognized. Some of the challenges come from 'within' when an individual is not properly 'grounded' in their realizations. But the foreknowledge is available to overcome or even avoid the possible pitfalls.

ESOTERIC CORRESPONDENCE.

Alternate Names : lois, ceridinen
Alphabet Letter : "L"
Ogma's Tree : "elm in the forests"
Alternate Trees : elm, mountain ash,
        red cedar, rosewood, the 'quick-

beam' tree

Bardic Value : 2 (duality and polarity; as above, so below); also the 'Great Division', heaven and earth, land and sea, the seen and unseen, &tc.

Alternative (R.Graves) : 14

Forest Rank (British) : Chieftain

Forest Rank (Irish) : Peasant

Quadratic Element : Air

Druid Guardian : Loth

Celtic Deities : Epona, Macha, Math; also Airmud (healing), Baile (communication), Beli (divination), Beltene (spirit contact), Borvo (healing), Caradoc (divination), Coll (astral), Crom Cruaich (spirits), Dhonn (past-lives), Grainne (astral), Gwendydd (divination) Gwyn ap Nudd (spirits), Oghma (communication), Rosmerta (communication), Taliesin (understanding time)

Druidic Deities : Llew (god of all crafts and trades), Llyr (sea, rain, waters), Laighinos (teacher of battle skills)

Solar Month : December

Lunar Month : January 21/22 – February 18;
Moon of Vision; Astral Travel Moon

Color Ogham : *liath*, gray, also red

Bird Ogham : *lachu*, duck

Sacred Animal : bear (the god, masculinity),
unicorn (the goddess, femininity)

Sacred Gems : smokey quartz, diamond,
yellow chrysolite, ruby

Ogham Forest Tract : personal empowerment,
protection against enchantment,
against control by others, astral or
otherworld (spirit world) work
(vision), patience, thoughtfulness,
'magical' work; planted outside the
front door to ward off negativity

Arts of Civilization : *lumnacht*, pilotage

DIVINATION SYMBOLISM.

Description : two notches to the right of the
stemline (or downward facing if a
horizontal stemline)

Word Ogham (Morann mac Main) : "Li sula—
delight of eye; the flame"

Word Ogham (Mac Ind Oic) : "Cara ceathra—
friend of cattle; quickening-tree"

Tarot Equivalent : The High Priest—open-
mindedness (or stubbornness, if
reversed), recognition of truth,
solidifying foundations

Ogham Lochlannach : *perth*—assertiveness,
karma, initiation; also 'pear tree';
abundance, luxury, display, lavish-
ness; also debauchery, decadence,
excess, gluttony; physical pleasure

Personality : spiritual
Inversion : fanatical

Oracular Meaning : awareness and insight
(inner understanding), self-control,
empowerment, protection and
nurturing (motherhood and father-
hood), evanescence, 'the tree of
quickening'

3. *fearn* — **alder tree**

> "Alder energy drives the warrior spirit, allowing
> one to stand fast in battle or conflict, or when
> confronted with an over-abundance of external
> pressures. Just as the head of Bran arrived in the
> midst of battle to reveal important prophecies,
> so must a wizard be open to the inner voice."
>
> —Joshua Free
> 'The Enchanted Forest'
> (Elvenomicon Series-I)

Having overcome challenges of starting up the path, a Seeker must maintain personal integrity in order to maintain their footholds upon it. This requires keeping aware of what's hidden beneath the surface all around us at all times. Rather than be 'on guard', we can simply increase our active awareness. In light of this, the Seeker may move ahead with utmost confidence and without the need to tread lightly and without succumbing to basic upsets.

ESOTERIC CORRESPONDENCE.

Alternate Names : fern
Alphabet Letter : "F"

Ogma's Tree : "alder in the forest"

Alternate Trees : maple

Bardic Value : 3 (triad, trinity, triangle); or 5 in some B-L-N systems (quintessence, Akasha)

  Alternative (R.Graves) : 8

Forest Rank (British) : Chieftain

Forest Rank (Irish) : Peasant

Quadratic Element : Fire

Druid Guardian : Forann

Celtic Deities : Bran ('The Blessed'), Macha; also Ambisagrus (weather), Arthur (self-sacrifice), Druantia (the ecosystem), Figol (patience), Fionn (overcoming), Leucetios (weather), Nomenoe (service to others), Owen Lawgoch (self-sacrifice), Pryderi (duty), Saba (ecology), Scathach (teaching), Stine Bheag (weather)

Druidic Deities : Fionn (architecture, strategy), Ffagus (the 'Beech god', forgotten knowledge, lore), Formorix (invention, sea/air travel)

Solar Month : January

Lunar Month : March 19 – April 15; Moon of

Utility, Moon of Efficacy, Moon of
Self-Guidance; or February 18 –
March 17 (in some tree calendars)

Color Ogham : *flann*, red, also crimson

Bird Ogham : *faelinn*, gull

Sacred Animal : fox (slyness, wit, cunning),
ram (achievement through per-
sonal sacrifice), raven (protection)

Sacred Gems : beryl, serpentine, fire-garnet,
obsidian

Ogham Forest Tract : charcoal, dye, housing
foundations, protection/defense,
foundation of wisdom/knowledge

Arts of Civilization : *filideacht*, bardic poetry

DIVINATION SYMBOLISM.

Description : three notches to the right of
the stemline (or downward facing if
a horizontal stemline)

Word Ogham (Morann mac Main) : "*Airinach
Fian*—shield of the warriors"

Word Ogham (Mac Ind Oic) : "*Comet Iachta*—
guarding of milk, for of alder are
made the vessels containing milk"

Tarot Equivalent : Strength—disillusionment,

need for organization, use of personal strength

Ogham Lochlannach : uruz—strength, manifestation, sacrifice; also 'aurochs'; masculinity, freedom, energy, action, courage; also lust, rashness, violence; sexual desire

Personality : ambitious
  Inversion : impulsive

Oracular Meaning : foundation, protection, guidance, resistance to water (or enchantment), shielding (overcoming difficulties, confronting), 'the tree of resistance' (inner strength)

4. *saille* — willow tree

"The noble willow, burn not, a tree sacred to poems; within his bloom bees are a-sucking, and all love the little cage."

—Iubhdan

The feminine grace of the willow tree has captivated artists and poets since ancient times. It speaks to us of the subtler aspects of life: the nighttime dreamscapes and otherworldly faerie realms. It speaks to us of intuition, and of the tendency inherent in the human condition to ignore the 'inner voice' that is actually our own, but which is often washed out by the hidden influences, imprinting and emotional encoding of living in a fragmented world. By learning to hear and listen to ourselves, free of what we have taken on and carried with us as a burden of experience, the self-confidence and determination necessary to move forward can be assured.

ESOTERIC CORRESPONDENCE.

Alternate Names : sail, awn, helyg, helygen, suil

Alphabet Letter : "S"

Ogma's Tree : "willow in the forest"

Alternate Trees : n/a

Bardic Value : 4 (the cosmic cube, solid); foundation of solid manifestation, the four directions

 Alternative (R.Graves) : 16

Forest Rank (British) : Chieftain

Forest Rank (Irish) : Peasant

Quadratic Element : Water

Druid Guardian : Saliath

Celtic Deities : Silver Huntress, Arianrhod, Diana ("of the Forest"), Epona; also Boann (fertility), Cerridwen (shape-shifting), Dana (elves/faerie), Fand (elves/faerie), Maeve (femininity), Nantosuelta (fertility), Nessa (femininity), Rhiannon (fertility), Sheila-na-gig (femininity), Taillte (fertility)

Druidic Deities : Samhann (god of death, guardian of the Otherworld gate), Sucellus (fighting, assassination), Silvanus (herb-lore, plants, healing)

Solar Month : February

Lunar Month : April 16 – May 12; the Witch's

Moon, Moon of Balance; March 18 –
April 14 (in some tree calenders)

Color Ogham : *sodath*, fine-coloured; also
fiery-coloured

Bird Ogham : *seg*, hawk (loftiness, nobility)

Sacred Animal : hare (intuition), cat (detach-
ment) and owl (wisdom)

Sacred Gems : opal, pearl, sugulite, uvulite,
peridot

Ogham Forest Tract : lunar magick, dream
work, femininity, fertility, healing,
baskets/wicker-work, Otherworld
contact, an aid to divination

Arts of Civilization : *sairsi*, handicraft

DIVINATION SYMBOLISM.

Description : four notches to the right of the
stemline (or downward facing if a
horizontal stemline)

Word Ogham (Morann mac Main) : "Li n-aimbi
—hue of the lifeless; of one dead"

Word Ogham (Mac Ind Oic) : "Luth bech—the
activity of bees"

Tarot Equivalent : The Moon—dreams,
hidden influences (hidden forces),

intuition needed, self-reliance required, forthcoming subtle changes

Ogham Lochlannach : *laguz*—lake life, flow,
fertility; also 'water'; river, ocean,
dreams, fantasies, mysteries, the
underworld; also madness, despair,
obsession, suicide; the unconscious

Personality : wise
  Inversion : bitter

Oracular Meaning : beauty, enchantment,
rhythm, cycles, harmony, inspiration, an indication that emotional
healing is necessary (confidence),
intuition, flexibility

5. *nuin* — **ash tree**

"You ash, cruel tree... turn not aside
A foot's-breadth ye, straight at the heart fly free.
Nuin Neiagadin—spear shaft be!"

—Song of the Forest Trees
(Monroe Version)

Ash represents the "combination" of factors involved—the systems that make up the System. In many ancient European traditions, the ash tree is the 'World Tree' or 'cosmic axis' that connects all 'worlds' or 'universes'. It is the link between the 'inner' and 'outer'—and demonstrates that they are one and the same; that what is going on 'out there' is not independent of what is going on 'in here'. The ash bridges the aspects of 'beingness' and 'doingness'.

ESOTERIC CORRESPONDENCE.

Alternate Names : nin, nwyn, nion

Alphabet Letter : "N"

Ogma's Tree : "maw of a spear, or nettles in the woods"

Alternate Trees : redbud, ponderosa pine

Bardic Value : 5 (control of the soul), or 3 (in some B-L-N systems)

  Alternative (R.Graves) : 13

Forest Rank (British) : Chieftain

Forest Rank (Irish) : Chieftain

Quadratic Element : Air

Druid Guardian : Nebgadon/Nebuchadnezzar

Celtic Deities : Lugh, Ogma, Woden/Odin, Gwydion; also Biddy Mamionn (healing), Habetrot (healing)

Druidic Deities : Nudd (the 'cloud-maker', weather, storms, seasons), Nuada (wealth, water, power, dominion), Nwyvre (stars and planets)

Solar Month : March

Lunar Month : February 19 – March 18; Moon of Waters; April 15 – May 12 (in some tree calenders)

Color Ogham : *necht*, clear; also clear-green

Bird Ogham : *nescu*, snipe

Sacred Animal : adder or serpent (healing, transformation, life-force)

Sacred Gems : sapphire, sea-green beryl, peridot, smithsonite

Ogham Forest Tract : maypoles, spears (also pool cues, paddles/oars) wands, sea/water magick, empowerment, healing, increase of personal ability

Arts of Civilization : *notaireacht*, notary

DIVINATION SYMBOLISM.

Description : five notches to the right of the stemline (or downward facing if a horizontal stemline)

Word Ogham (Morann mac Main) : "*Cosdad sida*—checking of peace; the maw of the weaver's beam"

Word Ogham (Mac Ind Oic) : "*Bag ban*—fight of women, to wit, a weaver's beam"

Tarot Equivalent : The World (Universe)— end of a cycle, freedom, perfection, satisfaction, success, triumph

Ogham Lochlannach : *algiz*—life, protection, meta-human; also 'aesir' or 'one of the gods'; goodness, health, truth, harmony, wisdom, insight; vanity

Personality : charming
  Inversion : egocentric

Oracular Meaning : triumph, protection,

overcoming mental strife and
boredom, change of outlook (view-
point), 'World Tree' (connection
between 'inner' and 'outer' worlds),
awakening, 'the tree of personal
strength', harmony (peace), rebirth

6. *huathe* — **hawthorn tree**

*"The power of 'H' is that it increases the power of
other letters in a grammatical context.
This applies equally on a spiritual level.
Once the magical or spiritual work is finished,
you must expect a period of disruption,
which should not be too severe or upsetting."*

—Steve Blamires
'Celtic Tree Mysteries'

Hawthorn begins the second *aicme* of five *fews* and represents the first challenges faced after this breakthrough on the pathway. Navigating safely through thorns requires patience, but is not impossible. Often these barriers are only erected to thwart those who have come this far on the journey from going further. But the passageway is much narrower than before—and as such, it requires that Seeker 'lighten their load' in order to proceed. The way ahead is only restricting when we have not adequately cleared away the debris.

ESOTERIC CORRESPONDENCE.

Alternate Names : huath, huatha
Alphabet Letter : "H"

Ogma's Tree : "test tree, or whitethorn"

Alternate Trees : whitethorn, sycamore, laurel, cottonwood

Bardic Value : 6 (time)

Forest Rank (British) : Peasant

Forest Rank (Irish) : Peasant

Quadratic Element : Fire

Druid Guardian : Huiria

Celtic Deities : Olwen, Hurle, Rhiannon; also Aine (summertime), Arianrhod (bindings), Lugh (fire)

Druidic Deities : Hagfgan (gems and stones), Hesus (prophecy, springs, caves), Heremonix (wells and underground rivers)

Solar Month : April

Lunar Month : May 13 – June 9/10; Moon of Restraint, Moon of Hindrance, the Summer Moon

Color Ogham : *huath*, terrible; also purple

Bird Ogham : *hadaig/aadaig*, night raven

Sacred Animal : goat (material life), dragon (power, vitality, energy)

Sacred Gems : amethyst, tanzanite, lapis

lazuli, carnelian

Ogham Forest Tract : hawthorn wood is not
usually taken; wands and wards are
cut between April 21 and May 1 for
love and magick marriage rites;
grown as a living being for general
'magical' protection and success

Arts of Civilization : *h-airchetul*, trisyllabic
poetry (triads ?)

DIVINATION SYMBOLISM.

Description : one notch to the left of the
stemline (or upward facing if a
horizontal stemline)

Word Ogham (Morann mac Main) : "*Conal cuan*
—a pack of wolves"

Word Ogham (Mac Ind Oic) : "*Banadh gnuisi*—
blanching of face in fear or terror"

Tarot Equivalent : Judgment—nearing completion, forthcoming renewal, look-
ing ahead, guidance needed

Ogham Lochlannach : *hagalz*—hail, disruption,
framework; also 'precipitation';
pain, loss, suffering, hardship, sick-
ness, natural disaster; also testing,

temptation; the 'Wrath of Nature'

Personality : passionate
  Inversion : ruthless

Oracular Meaning : purity, restraint (being
    held back for a time), chastity
    (similar to the white-'heather'
    Ogham); also love and marriage
    proper (marital pleasure), prosper-
    ity, challenges (harshness, misfort-
    une), healing of the heart (love)

7. *duir* — oak tree

*"When the beech prospers through spells and
litanies, the oak-tops entangle,
there is hope for the trees.
With foot-beat of the swift oak, the heavens
and earth rung; stout 'guardian of the door',
his name in every tongue."*

—Robert Graves
'Battle of the Trees'

Having passed through the thorn barrier, oak trees represent the enduring strength that is achieved. Oak signifies the layers of knowingness or realization—of which "Druids" named themselves after. Even thin layers combined will generate solidity. Universally, oak trees stand as the 'doorways' or 'gateways' of time and space—and thus a continuum to the past and future that is accessible to a Seeker. In these cases, the oak represents the "doors of perception."

ESOTERIC CORRESPONDENCE.

Alternate Names : dur, dwyr, derwen, dar,
        doir
Alphabet Letter : "D"

Ogma's Tree : "oak in the forest"

Alternate Trees : hickory, western cedar, sequoia; also related to 'holly' ogham

Bardic Value : 7 (lunar or faerie, dreams or enchantments); also, perfected knowledge of the local universe (seven days, seven ancient planets)

  Alternative (R.Graves) : 12

Forest Rank (British) : Peasant

Forest Rank (Irish) : Chieftain

Quadratic Element : Fire

Druid Guardian : Daivaith (Dagda)

Celtic Deities : Belinos; also Abelard (loyalty), Awawen (friendship/loyalty), Artio (fertility), Cernunnos (the forest), Connla (wisdom, loyalty), Dagda (masculinity), Laeg (loyalty), Llewellyn (elves/faerie), Merlin (magic), Rohand (duty/loyalty)

Druidic Deities : Dagda (the 'Good God', 'All-Father', god of Druidism), Dian Cecht (healing), Dis Pater ('oldest grandfather of the races')

Solar Month : May

Lunar Month : June 10/11 – July 7; Moon of

Strength, Moon of Security

Color Ogham : *dub*, black; also dark-brown

Bird Ogham : *droeii*, wren (the "druid's bird")

Sacred Animal : white mare (the earth/land), lion/tiger (sovereignty), salamander, adder-serpent

Sacred Gems : yellow topaz, amber, gold, white carnelian, moonstone

Ogham Forest Tract : doors (protection for homes), fertility; '*galls*' used for the '*naddred*' talisman (Adder's Egg or Druid's Gem), Druidic spirituality

Arts of Civilization : *druidheacht*, wizardry

DIVINATION SYMBOLISM.

Description : two notches to the left of the stemline (or upward facing if a horizontal stemline)

Word Ogham (Morann mac Main) : "*Ardavi dossaibh*—highest of bushes"

Word Ogham (Mac Ind Oic) : "*Gres sair*—carpenter's work"

Tarot Equivalent : Emperor—exterior authority, inner balance, responsibility, use of experience

Ogham Lochlannach : *thurisa*—gateway, door,
defense; also 'Thor' or 'thunder';
also evil, malice, hatred, torment,
lies; but also catharsis, cleansing,
purging; a malevolent individual

Personality : fatherly

Inversion : dominating

Oracular Meaning : protection, strength, a
'doorway' (to personal growth),
sovereignty, guidance, endurance,
higher powers at work, security,
truth, the 'King of the Woods'

8. *tinne* — **holly tree**

> *"The holly, dark and green, made a resolute*
> *stand; armed with many spear-points*
> *wounding the hand."*
>
> —Robert Graves
> 'The Battle of the Trees'

Once a Seeker has broken through initial barriers and solidified their position, it is a time for *action*. But it also requires that one is clear about their endeavors before pursuing them. In some ways, holly represents the balance of forces through *action*—the inertia and resonance that ensues—and manifests visibly as movement through 'actions' and corresponding 'reactive' courses of motion. Like the oak, holly represents endurance, but of activity—and as an evergreen, signifies actively holding up against harshness and tests of strength.

ESOTERIC CORRESPONDENCE.

Alternate Names : celynen

Alphabet Letter : "T"

Ogma's Tree : "holly, or elderberry in the
   forest"

Alternate Trees : black walnut, holly-oak

Bardic Value : 8 (purification, the annual cycle or 'wheel-of-the-year'); also the 'magnificence of the sun'

  Alternative (R.Graves) : 11

Forest Rank (British) : Peasant

Forest Rank (Irish) : Chieftain

Quadratic Element : Fire

Druid Guardian : Teilmon

Celtic Deities : The Holly King (Holly-Man), Cu Chulain (strength); also Cernunnos (fertility); Dahud (sexuality), Fergus (sexuality), Flidais (animals), Guildeluec (choices), Macha (wisdom)

Druidic Deities : Taranis (the 'Thunderer'), Tigernonos (hills, mountains and valleys), Toutorix (war, power)

Solar Month : June

Lunar Month : July 8 – August 4; Moon of Encirclement, Moon of Polarity

Bird Ogham : *truith*, starling

Color Ogham : *tenien*, dark gray

Sacred Animal : warhorse (protection), warhound (loyalty)

Sacred Gems : ruby, rose quartz, blue topaz

Ogham Forest Tract : spear-making (combat and protection), chariot wheels, charcoal; grown to bring good fortune and ward off evil

Arts of Civilization : *tornoracht*, turning (?)

DIVINATION SYMBOLISM.

Description : three notches to the left of the stemline (or upward facing if a horizontal stemline)

Word Ogham (Morann mac Main) : "*Trian*— 'another thing', the meaning of that today"

Word Ogham (Mac Ind Oic) : "*Smir guaili*— fires of coal"

Tarot Equivalent : The Chariot—application of energy, movement, travel, self-discipline, triumph, success

Ogham Lochlannach : *ehwaz*—movement, soul travel; also 'horse'; transport-ation, speed, a vehicle; also haste, blind rushing in; rapid progress

Personality : determined
  Inversion : insensitive

Oracular Meaning : movement, vigorous
action, vitality, energy, holiness
(sacredness), 'lifeforce', natural
cycles, a path between extremes
(balance), the 'survivor tree'

9. *coll* – **hazel tree**

> *"Why is the crane in the next place?*
> *Not hard. This is the month of wisdom,*
> *and the wisdom of Mannan Mac Lir,*
> *namely the Beth-Luis-Nion [Ogham],*
> *was wrapped in Crane-skin.*
> *And brown are the nuts of the Hazel,*
> *the tree of wisdom."*
>
> —Robert Graves
> 'The White Goddess'

The hazel tree symbolizes not only an acquisition of arcane knowledge and ancient wisdom but also its comprehension and communication. Synthesis and communicability of data is necessary for its effective use for any application—otherwise it simply remains in a pool of potential. The hazel tree and its nut represent pursuit of that potential and practical integration for a continuing existence. Hazel may also signify that divine guidance is at hand or attainable.

ESOTERIC CORRESPONDENCE.

Alternate Names : koll, calltuinn
Alphabet Letter : "C" and "K"

Ogma's Tree : "hazel"

Alternate Trees : nut-hazel, beech, pecan, white-oak

Bardic Value : 9 (the completion of wisdom and knowledge)

Forest Rank (British) : Peasant

Forest Rank (Irish) : Chieftain

Quadratic Element : Water

Druid Guardian : Kay (Cai)

Celtic Deities : Llyr, Branwen; also Bebhionn (spirits), Ban Naomha (wisdom), Cailleach (wisdom), Pwyll (justice)

Druidic Deities : Cernunnos (the 'Horned-One', animals, deep forests), Cromm Cruaich (darkness, death), Camulos (Mars, war, blood, conquest)

Solar Month : July

Lunar Month : August 5 – September 1; the Moon of the Wise, the Crone Moon

Color Ogham : *cron*, brown

Bird Ogham : *corr*, crane (hidden knowledge, patience, longevity)

Sacred Animal : *bradan*, salmon (wisdom, inspiration)

Sacred Gems : lapis lazuli, sapphire, opal, banded red agate, magnetite

Ogham Forest Tract : wands, baskets, thatch-work, divination sticks; nuts used for love spells and potions to aid inducing 'spirit vision', inspiration

Arts of Civilization : *cruitireacht*, harping

DIVINATION SYMBOLISM.

Description : four notches to the left of the stemline (or upward facing if a horizontal stemline)

Word Ogham (Morann mac Main) : "*Cainiu fedaib*—fairest of trees, owing to its beauty in the woods"

Word Ogham (Mac Ind Oic) : "*Cara bloisc*—friend of cracking"

Tarot Equivalent : The High Priestess—inspiration, intuition, spiritual connectedness, uncovering hidden influences

Ogham Lochlannach : *othila*—property and prosperity; also 'heritage' (estate); house, land of birth (mother land); also what one is 'bound' to

Personality : generous
  Inversion : deceptive

Oracular Meaning : divination (oracles),
    creativity (inspiration), intuition,
    spirit vision or inner vision, true
    sight (skrying), wisdom, knowledge,
    productivity (nut-bearing), insight
    (perceptions), the "poet's tree"

10. *quert* — **apple tree**

"Sweet apple tree growing by the river,
Who will thrive on its wondrous fruit?
When my reason was intact, I used to lie at its
foot with a fair wanton maiden of slender form."

—Myrddin the Bard
'Black Book of Carmarthen'

On the pursuit toward wholeness, apples signify the 'fruits-gained'. Fulfillment of wholeness at the level of material existence is often identified with companionate love as a means of correcting the symmetry of our own personal fragmentation. So while we are able to reach states of happiness and recognize the beauty in the world, we are also susceptible to misappropriating the sensory sensual fulfillment of this world as a substitute for the inner calling to reconnect our awareness and consciousness with the spiritual-Self that is eternal and superior to all human experience.

ESOTERIC CORRESPONDENCE.

Alternate Names : queris
Alphabet Letter : "Q"

Ogma's Tree : "quickening tree, or aspen"

Alternate Trees : crab-apple, orange

Bardic Value : 10 (the 'Divine Completion');
      red. 1; or often unnumbered (as in
      the tree calendar count, &tc.)

Forest Rank (British) : Peasant

Forest Rank (Irish) : Chieftain

Quadratic Element : Water

Druid Guardian : Qualep

Celtic Deities : Kerridwen (or Cerridwen),
      Mannan mac Lyr

Druidic Deities : Affalon

Solar Month : n/a

Lunar Month : sometimes August 5 –
      September 1; sometimes not
      included in the calendar; also
      September 2 – September 29 (in
      some tree calenders)

Color Ogham : *quiar*, mouse-coloured; also
      green

Bird Ogham : *querc*, hen (femininity)

Sacred Animal : unicorn (beauty, purity,
      enchantment)

Sacred Gems : rose quartz, amethyst

Ogham Forest Tract : food (fruit), drink (cider), the 'apple-wand' or 'silver-branch', healing, link to the Otherworld

Arts of Civilization : *quislenacht*, fluting

DIVINATION SYMBOLISM.

Description : five notches to the left of the stemline (or upward facing if a horizontal stemline)

Word Ogham (Morann mac Main) : "*Clithar mbaiscaill*—shelter of a hind, i.e., 'a fold'; to wit, *boscell*, lunatic; that is *bas-ceall*, death sense, the sense that comes when one goes to their death"

Word Ogham (Mac Ind Oic) : "*Brigh an duine*—force of a man"

Tarot Equivalent : The Empress—fertility, growth, joy, prosperity, satisfaction

Ogham Lochlannach : *berkana*—birth, life, growth; also 'birch tree'; fertility, healing; also desire, passion, carelessness; a love affair or new birth

Personality : motherly

Inversion : weak-willed

Oracular Meaning : love, beauty, unity of
mind and spirit between lovers,
eternal life (perpetual youth),
abundance, fertility, healing,
personal wholeness (development
or completion of spiritual work),
sometimes indicates 'choices'

11. *muin* — **vine**

*"Muin represents hidden, just below-the-surface
realizations, sometimes only brought to the
surface when disinhibited—that which cannot
be healthily suppressed if we are to break through
to the next steps of our progression.
With an ability to even scale walls,
the Vine truly knows no boundaries."*

—Joshua Free
'The Enchanted Forest'
(Elevenomicon Series-I)

The vine leads off the third *aicme* with a moment of inwardness and introspection. This does not mean introversion or inactivity, and quite the contrary, the vine represents realizing and removing personal inhibitions that cause one to withhold energies and thereby withdraw outward participation in creation of reality. Naturally, the vine also warns against the dangers of drunken excess and extremes in this same regard.

ESOTERIC CORRESPONDENCE.

Alternate Names : min, gwynwydden
Alphabet Letter : M

Ogma's Tree : "vine, or mead"

Alternate Trees : mulberry, grape, blackberry
(also the elm, a tree used in Britain
to support the vines)

Bardic Value : 10 (prophecy) or 11 if previous
'apple' is numbered, &tc.; *red.* 1 or 2
(though some numerologic schools
don't reduce elevens, if counted 11)

  Alternative (R.Graves) : 6

Forest Rank (British) : Shrub

Forest Rank (Irish) : Shrub (?)

Quadratic Element : Water

Druid Guardian : Muriath

Celtic Deities : Brigantia; also Brid (protection), Caer (dreams), Epona (dreams)

Druidic Deities : Mabon (the 'divine youth',
music, poetry, beauty), Math (mag-
ic, shapeshifting), Myrddin (magic)

Solar Month : August

Lunar Month : September 2 – September 29;
Moon of Celebration; September 30
– October 27 (in some tree calend-
ers)

Color Ogham : *mbracht*, variegated

Bird Ogham : *mintan*, titmouse (survival)

Sacred Animal : scorpion, lizard, serpent

Sacred Gems : aquamarine, amethyst, yellow serpentine, jasper

Ogham Forest Tract : grape-wine, intoxication, meditation, revealing truths, harvest (manifestation)

Arts of Civilization : *milaideacht*, soldiering

DIVINATION SYMBOLISM.

Description : one long notch diagonally intersecting across the stemline

Word Ogham (Morann mac Main) : "*Tresim fedma*—strongest of effort, i.e., the back of a man or ox"

Word Ogham (Mac Ind Oic) : "*Arusc n-airlig*— condition of slaughter, to wit, a man's back"

Tarot Equivalent : The Lovers—changes, determination, possible indication of relationship (romantic love)

Ogham Lochlannach : *gebo*—partnership, sexuality, lovers; also 'gift'; award, inheritance; but also sacrifice

Personality : sympathetic
  Inversion : dependent

Oracular Meaning : inner-development, self-
realization (introspection, inwardness), hidden knowledge (prophecy), comprehension, manifestation
(harvest)

12. *gort* — **ivy**

*"Around the ivy path, the Autumn
turns the trees aflame with color.
Taliesin, wise man fleeing
from the wrath of Cauldron Mother."*

—The Roebuck in the Thicket
(Robert Graves)

Ivy represents inner growth and development
such as is depicted in its spiral-like pattern. It
also signifies abilities to overcome obstacles,
even scaling walls. Its ability to scale walls is
dependent on there being a wall present to
assist. This reminds us not to be afraid to lean
on good solid support when it can be found. It
must be quality support, however, because as
one progresses along the pathway of Ascension there are those that will be envious or
jealous, and this is sometimes demonstrated
in 'false help'—even when it occurs subcon-
sciously and not blatant malicious attacks.

ESOTERIC CORRESPONDENCE.

Alternate Names : uruin, eiddew
Alphabet Letter : "G"

Ogma's Tree : "cornfield, or fir in the forest"

Alternate Trees : elm, blackberry (although also associated with 'vine' Ogham)

Bardic Value : 11 (maternity) or 12 (if using the alternative count); *red.* 2 or 3; though some numerologic schools don't reduce elevens)

Alternative (R.Graves) : 10

Forest Rank (British) : Shrub

Forest Rank (Irish) : Shrub

Quadratic Element : Earth

Druid Guardian : Gahth

Celtic Deities : Swan Maidens, Cuchulain, Cernunnos/Kernunnos, Orion, Ogmios; also Brian Boru (leadership), Bres (compassion), Melusine (compassion), Niamh (leadership), Veleda (leadership)

Druidic Deities : Govannon ('divine smith', metalcraft), Gwyn ap Nudd (god of 'the Wild Hunt'), Grannos (corn, harvest)

Solar Month : September

Lunar Month : September 30 – October 27; Moon of Buoyancy, Moon of

Resilience; October 28 – November
24 (in some tree calenders)

Color Ogham : *gorm*, blue; also sky-blue

Bird Ogham : *ge'is*, swan or "mute swan"
(love, partnership, community)

Sacred Animal : boar (leadership, focus,
the 'warrior')

Sacred Gems : chryso(beryl), green jasper,
clear green jasper

Ogham Forest Tract : exorcisms/banishings,
encouragement (support), determination

Arts of Civilization : *gaibneacht*, smithwork

DIVINATION SYMBOLISM.

Description : two long notches diagonally
intersecting across the stemline

Word Ogham (Morann mac Main) : "*Milisiu
feraib*—sweeter than grass; the
cornfield"

Word Ogham (Mac Ind Oic) : "*Med nercc*—ivy"

Tarot Equivalent : Justice—the consideration
of all factors (equality and fairness),
possible outside factors

Ogham Lochlannach : *teiwaz*—gods judgment, warrior justice; also 'Tiwaz' (deity); victory, battle, winning disputes

Personality : ambitious
  Inversion : lazy

Oracular Meaning : cooperation, community (support), healing, 'inner-spiral' (journey), restrictions (warnings), development (new skills, &tc.), taking time to consider all aspects

13. *ngetal* – reeð

"You reed, swift to pursue...
Skillful and slender, straight never-bending.
Ngetal Ngoimar—fly ever-true!"
—Song of the Forest Trees
(Monroe Version)

Ancient Mesopotamians employed the reed to fashion their stylus-pens and manage literary communication. This is relevant to the Ogham because the "ng" *few* seems to have only been adopted to preserve writing in languages other than Celtic. Whether reed or broom, this Ogham represents a communication of knowledge—which also means application of knowledge or 'doingness'. Personal confidence in one's own Self-determination is dependent on maintaining elevated states of knowingness. It is only when in doubt—or enshrouded in mystery—that a person hesitates, falters, or otherwise lingers in a realm of maybe.

ESOTERIC CORRESPONDENCE.

Alternate Names : getal, corsen, erun
Alphabet Letter : "Ng"

Ogma's Tree : "broom"

Alternates : cattail, horsetail, broom, fern

Bardic Value : 12 (divine or royal purposes),
or 13 if using alternative count; *red.*
3 or 4 (depending on which count
and if reduced)

Forest Rank (British) : Shrub

Forest Rank (Irish) : Shrub (?)

Quadratic Element : Air

Druid Guardian : Noimahr

Celtic Deities : Olbaal, Gwydion, Morgana,
Morrighan; also Bran (divination),
Coventina (divination), Don (fam-
ily)

Druidic Deities : Arianrhod

Solar Month : October

Lunar Month : October 28 – October 30 (the
three days before *Samhain*); the
Moon of the Home, Hearth Moon,
Winter Moon, the Moon which
Manifests Truth; also November 25
– December 23 (in some tree calen-
ders)

Color Ogham : *nglas*, grass-green

Bird Ogham : *ngeigh*, goose (parental-style

vigilance, reproduction)

Sacred Animal : stag (independence, pride), dog, rat, owl

Sacred Gems : aquamarine

Ogham Forest Tract : writing pens, brooms, pipes, fertility/love magick

Arts of Civilization : *ngibae*, modeling

DIVINATION SYMBOLISM.

Description : three long notches diagonally intersecting across the stemline

Word Ogham (Morann mac Main) : "*Luth legha*—a physician's strength"

Word Ogham (Mac Ind Oic) : "*Eitiud midach*—a physician's robe"

Tarot Equivalent : Wheel of Fortune—the ups and downs of life, chance, cycles, opportunity, randomness (the randomity of life / the 'life game')

Ogham Lochlannach : raido—right action and movement; also 'ride' or 'journey'; travel, relocation, evolution, transportation; but also disruption, dislocation

Personality : adaptable

Inversion : indecisive

Oracular Meaning : effort (direct action),
application (of effort or intention),
further work needed for completion, clearing away the old to make
way for what is necessary to finish,
harmony

14. *straif* — **blackthorn tree**

*"The surly blackthorn is a wanderer,
and a wood that the artificer burns not;
throughout his body, though it be scanty,
birds in their flocks warble."*

—Iubhdan

Blackthorn is often slighted out as a negative Ogham due to its association with *control*. And most individuals have had poor experiences with 'enforced control' and unwanted outside influence. The blackthorn represents another significant energetic barrier on the Pathway, whereby a Seeker must shed the conditioned and imprinted influences and enforced command from outside sources. Often times these commands are imprinted into circuits that an individual keeps on following long after the fact.

While there is some benefit to social education (and observational learning) when one is seeking to fit into a society, the manner in which we become entrapped to a human condition and victims to this world is taking things a step too far.

ESOTERIC CORRESPONDENCE.

Alternate Names : straife, strife

Alphabet Letter : "ST"/"Z" and "STR"

Ogma's Tree : "willow-brake in the forest"

Alternate Trees : plum ('*emrys*')

Bardic Value : 14 when using alternate count; *red.* 5; or often unnumbered

Forest Rank (British) : Shrub

Forest Rank (Irish) : Shrub

Quadratic Element : Earth

Druid Guardian : Stru

Celtic Deities : Taliesin

Druidic Deities : Scathach, Skadi

Solar Month : n/a

Lunar Month : October 31 (*Samhain festival*); more often not included in the calendar

Color Ogham : *sorcha*, bright; also 'bright purple'

Bird Ogham : *stniolach*, thrush

Sacred Animal : wolf (the mysterious), toad (hidden power), black cat (sensitivity, intuition)

Sacred Gems : obsidian

Ogham Forest Tract : the 'Thunder and Lightning' Staff, the 'Dark Staff' a.k.a. *Shillelagh*, cudgel weapons, warding against evil and illness, channeling 'magical' power

Arts of Civilization : *streghuindeacht*, deer-stalking

DIVINATION SYMBOLISM.

Description : four long notches diagonally intersecting across the stemline

Word Ogham (Morann mac Main) : "*Tresiiu ruamna*—strongest of red, sloe red for dyeing things"

Word Ogham (Mac Ind Oic) : "*Morad run*—increasing of secrets, to wit, sloe"

Tarot Equivalent : Temperance—balance, seek harmony and security, a possible indication to slow down and 'temper' emotions

Ogham Lochlannach : *daguz*—prosperity, breakthrough; also 'daylight'; a day or cycle, period, span of time; also full circuit (full circle); completion

Personality : honest
  Inversion : deceptive
Oracular Meaning : cleansing, control,
           operating by force, confusion,
           restraint (constraint), resentment,
           coercion, threats, aggression,
           sudden change, renewal, strife,
           protection, stillness, severity, fate

15. *ruis* — **elder tree**

> "*Stoop not down afar, for a precipice lies
> below the earth: fearful depths drawing down
> through the ladder which has seven steps.
> Beneath which stands the throne of necessity.*"
>
> —The Oracle of the Elder Tree
> (Monroe Version)

The elder tree stands at the end of the third *aicme* representing the completion of a cycle, transitions and/or initiation into a final phase of work. Before reaching forward to the next level, a Seeker must release themselves from the 'ties that bind' in order for their chance at the ultimate 'redemption'. This involves the forgiveness of others in addition to one's self. Some method of personal 'reconciliation' or pastoral confession may be found in virtually all spiritual traditions—and for good reason. Only when an individual is able and prepared to face (or confront) their past head on will they be truly free from its hold.

ESOTERIC CORRESPONDENCE.

Alternate Names : ysgawen
Alphabet Letter : "R"

Ogma's Tree : "elder"

Alternate Trees : bourtree, hickory, myrtle, persimmon

Bardic Value : 13 (rebirth and transmigration), or 15 in the alternate count; *red.* 4 or 6

Forest Rank (British) : Shrub

Forest Rank (Irish) : Shrub

Quadratic Element : Earth

Druid Guardian : Ruben

Celtic Deities : Boann, Niknevin; also Balor (protection), Diancecht (healing), Gwyddion (wisdom), Meg (healing)

Druidic Deities : Ronanorix (death, old age), Rhonabwy (dreams, prophecy), Ruadanos (travel, crossroads)

Solar Month : "the '13th' month" ('*Samhain*')

Lunar Month : November; Moon of Completeness; not included in some tree calender counts

Color Ogham : *ruadh*, red ("blood red")

Bird Ogham : *rocnat*, small rook

Sacred Animal : badger (prudence, planning), black sow (abundance, nourishment)

Sacred Gems : bloodstone, red jasper,
dark green malachite

Ogham Forest Tract : exorcism, banishing,
regeneration magick, elderberry
wine, faerie-sight oinment, healing,
sacrifice, inspiration

Arts of Civilization : *ronaireacht*, dispensing

DIVINATION SYMBOLISM.

Description : five long notches diagonally
intersecting across the stemline

Word Ogham (Morann mac Main) : "*Timieui
rucce*—intensest of blushes, that is
elderberry, to wit, the reddening or
shame that grows in a man's face"

Word Ogham (Mac Ind Oic) : "*Ruanma dreach*—
redness of face, to wit, blushing"

Tarot Equivalent : The Hanged Man—the
need for foresight, changing direction (or indecision), transition (mid-
life crisis), self-sacrifice

Ogham Lochlannach : *isa*—concentration and
standstill; also 'ice'; treachery,
illusion, deceit, betrayal, ambush,
plots; also allure, seduction, entrap-

ment; a cunning beautiful woman

Personality : intelligent
  Inversion : unfortunate

Oracular Meaning : self-reflection (self-examination), change, end of a cycle (completion, evolution), crossroads (toward a next level)

16. *ailim* — silver-fir tree

"You fir, uncouth and savage...
Untamed wood, you smash and ravage.
Ailim Achab—Be deadly in your mirth."
—Battle of the Forest Trees
(Monroe Version)

Having overcome our emotional encoding and feelings of guilt and betrayal, a new leg of the journey opens up to us as the fourth *aicme*. It is epitomized by the 'objectivity' maintained when one is freed up of artificial personality programming and filters that hinder the crystal clarity that is possible when viewing from Self and without fragmentation. Clearheadedness is imbued in the aura of firs and pines, which is probably why so many are instinctively drawn to these forests when the need to "center" or be "grounded" arises.

ESOTERIC CORRESPONDENCE.

Alternate Names : ailim, elma, ffynidwydden, pinwydden
Alphabet Letter : "A"
Ogma's Tree : "Scots-pine"

Alternate Trees : pine, elm, redwood, fir

Bardic Value : 16 ; *red.* 7; or often unnumbered

Forest Rank (British) : Bramble

Forest Rank (Irish) : Chieftain

Quadratic Element : Earth

Druid Guardian : Achab

Celtic Deities : Horned-Man (the Green-Man), Merlyn (Myrddin), Abban, Sezh, Arianrhod, Am-Mesh (Gaea), Cernunnos/Kernunnos

Druidic Deities : Amaethon (agriculture), Arawn ('otherworld king', hunting, hounds, the hunt/pursuit), Albiorix (poetry, orchards, streams)

Solar Month : n/a

Lunar Month : Winter Solstice (Yule festival)

Color Ogham : *alad*, piebald, speckled; also pale blue

Bird Ogham : *aidhircleog*, lapwing

Sacred Animal : cow or "red cow", stag or deer (independence, self-reliance)

Sacred Gems : agate (moss agate), clear quartz, tourmaline

Ogham Forest Tract : forest magick of all

kinds, earth memory, teaching,
sacred fires, the elves (elvenkind,
otherkin faerie)

Arts of Civilization : *airigeacht*, sovereignty

DIVINATION SYMBOLISM.

Description : one long notch perpendicular
across the stemline

Word Ogham (Morann mac Main) : "*Ardam
iachtadh*—loudest of groanings,
that is, groaning of disease, or
wondering, that is, marveling at
whatever circumstance"

Word Ogham (Mac Ind Oic) : "*Tosach fregra*—
beginning of an answer; the first
expression of every human being
after their birth"

Tarot Equivalent : The Devil (Horned-One)—
arrogance, bondage, egotism, pride,
materialism, need for self-control

Ogham Lochlannach : *nauthiz*—constraint,
persistence, deliverance; also need;
necessity, want, poverty, emotional
hunger; also resistance, survival;
defiance of circumstances

Personality : outgoing
  Inversion : introverted
Oracular Meaning : ancient knowledge, primal power, high views (objectivity, far sight, perspective, broad range of experience, new realizations), penetration, strength, 'the tree of leadership' (reign, vigor)

17. *ohn* — ᚠ**urze**

"The nature of divine growth
is neither stern nor savage, but alluring and calm.
It causes not fear in those subjected to it, but
attracts all things by persuasion and sympathy."

—Oracle of the Sweet Furze
(Monroe Version)

The furze or gorse Ogham represents the synthesis of information into *wisdom*. This means the illumination or true enlightenment that is sought or promised in all spiritual paths, but of which the Seeker seldom reaches their desired destination. At this point of the journey along the Ogham pathway—or up the ladder of learning—the destination is in sight and assured so long as the individual uses what they know to the best of their advantage.

ESOTERIC CORRESPONDENCE.

Alternate Names : onn, oir, piswydden
Alphabet Letter : "O"
Ogma's Tree : "furze, or ash"
Alternate Trees : gorse, spindle ('*gwyrthed*'),
        linden, basswood, silver-spruce,

lime

Bardic Value : 17 ; *red.* 8; or often unnumbered

Forest Rank (British) : Bramble

Forest Rank (Irish) : Bramble

Quadratic Element : Fire

Druid Guardian : Oise

Celtic Deities : Lugh, Llew, Adraste

Druidic Deities : Ogma (eloquence, literature, writing/scripts), Ossian ('beautiful youth', swordplay), Owein ap Urien (leadership, war, reincarnation)

Solar Month : n/a

Lunar Month : Spring Equinox (March 21)

Color Ogham : odhar, dun; also yellow and gold

Bird Ogham : odoroscrach, scrat

Sacred Animal : rabbits (rebirth), bees (organization, community)

Sacred Gems : peridot, green quartz, jade, emerald

Ogham Forest Tract : honey and food for animals, fertility, eroticism, purification

Arts of Civilization : *ogmoracht*, harvesting

DIVINATION SYMBOLISM.

Description : two long notches perpendicular across the stemline

Word Ogham (Morann mac Main) : "*Conguaui-aid echraidc*—helper of horses, to wit, the *ennaid* of the chariot, i.e., the wheels of a chariot"

Word Ogham (Mac Ind Oic) : "*Fethim saire*—smoothest of work, i.e., stone"

Tarot Equivalent : The Sun—happiness, joy, brilliance, brightness, blessings, fulfillment, honesty

Ogham Lochlannach : *sowelu*—wholeness, victory; also 'sun'; power, flaming-sword, cleansing fire; also justice, destruction; 'Wrath of God'

Personality : prosperous
  Inversion : vane

Oracular Meaning : wisdom, spiritual fulfill-ment, optimism, projection (like rays) and protection, sometimes indicates discovery of new inform-ation, synthesis of information

18. ur – **heather**

> *"There are two types of heather—red and white.
> Red-heather attracts passion and is a symbol
> of sexual energy and lust, whereas
> White-heather wards against passion and sex
> and symbolizes purity and chastity."*
>
> —Joshua Free
> 'The Enchanted Forest'
> (Elvenomicon Series-I)

The types of heather—red and white—represent the ultimate dilemma of continuation in material existence: reproduction versus personal immortality.

During the course of one's life, the focus is generally on one or the other. In terms of material evolution: when environmental factors are favorable, life will usually choose reproduction; but when they are particularly turbulent, the emphasis is generally on one's own survival, growth and progression along a pathway that traverses lifetimes beyond just *this* one. In the end, we are left with ourselves, whether or not we produce offspring along the way—which means that ultimately, the quest must be to secure our own immortality.

ESOTERIC CORRESPONDENCE.

Alternate Names : uir, uchelwydd (mistletoe)
  [although 'mistletoe' is treated as a
  "blank" Ogham stick for divination]

Alphabet Letter : "U"

Ogma's Tree : "thorn"

Alternate Trees : silver-poplar, 'mistletoe'

Bardic Value : 18 ; *red.* 9; or often unnumbered

Forest Rank (British) : Bramble

Forest Rank (Irish) : Bramble

Quadratic Element : Air

Druid Guardian : Uriath

Celtic Deities : Grainne, Bloddwedd, Freya

Druidic Deities : Uath mac Imoman (the 'son
  of terror', ancient magic), Urias
  (ancient wisdom, supreme knowledge), Uaithne Umai (pipes, harps,
  music)

Solar Month : n/a

Lunar Month : Summer Solstice ; or the day
  after Winter Solstice (for mistletoe)

Color Ogham : *usgdha*, resinous; also purple

Bird Ogham : *uiseog*, lark

Sacred Animal : bee, lion

Sacred Gems : amethyst, peridot, amertine

Ogham Forest Tract : healing, attracting rain, perfume (heather), the 'goddess'

Arts of Civilization : *umaideacht*, brasswork

DIVINATION SYMBOLISM.

Description : three long notches perpendicular across the stemline

Word Ogham (Morann mac Main) : "*Uaraib adbaib*—in cold dwellings, to wit, fresh; for from *uir*, the mould of the earth is *uaraib adbaib*"

Word Ogham (Mac Ind Oic) : "*Silad clann*—growing of plants, that is from *uir*, the soil of the earth"

Tarot Equivalent : The Fool (Heather current) —decisions, crossroads, taking measure before acting, new starts; or The Hermit (Mistletoe current) —experimentation, guidance, true wisdom, withdrawal (reclusive)

Ogham Lochlannach : *mannaz*—the self (on a path); also 'man' or 'humans'; skill, ability, craft, intelligence; also cun-

ning, slyness, craftiness, calculating
(the 'Magician')

Personality : carefree
  Inversion : superficial

Oracular Meaning : clarity, understanding
        the 'inner self' (heather), healing
        (mistletoe, the 'all-heal'), personal
        development (success, gain)

19. *eadha* — **poplar (aspen)**

> *"The danger that you must guard against,*
> *even at this level of attainment, is falling into*
> *the trap of self-importance. Realize that you*
> *are still capable of falling from grace,*
> *of making mistakes, of upsetting the delicate*
> *balance of things, when you do what you*
> *want rather than what you will."*
>
> —Steve Blamires
> 'Celtic Tree Mysteries'

Nearing the end of our journey on this cycle, the aspen tree stands to give us the final test of our convictions—but it also represents the strength to overcome all final obstacles and barriers to our ultimate success. Its presence urges the Seeker to 'push ahead' to the end, which is surely in sight at this juncture. Fears of success—whatever those last pieces are that keeps us from accomplishment—are met and faced or confronted dauntlessly. There is no fear of 'losing' anything because Self will remain.

ESOTERIC CORRESPONDENCE.

Alternate Names : edad, ebad, eubh, aethin,

k'emmir, beith-bhog

Alphabet Letter : "E"

Ogma's Tree : "yew"/"aspen"

Alternate Trees : aspen, white poplar, cottonwood

Bardic Value : 19 (or 21 as mistletoe); *red.* 10 or 1 (or *red.* 3 as mistletoe); or often unnumbered

Forest Rank (British) : Bramble

Forest Rank (Irish) : Shrub

Quadratic Element : Water

Druid Guardian : Essu

Celtic Deities : Brighid, Rhiannon, Keyne, Llyr

Druidic Deities : Eochaid Ollathar (the 'great horse father', animals), Esus (god of woodcutters and weaponry), Ethniu (language, speech)

Solar Month : n/a

Lunar Month : Autumn Equinox

Color Ogham : *erc*, red; also silver

Bird Ogham : *ela*, swan (love)

Sacred Animal : white mare (the goddess); also the serpent-snake (in some traditions)

Sacred Gems : gray topaz, opal, sapphire, citrine quartz

Ogham Forest Tract : shapeshifting, shields, divination, 'rites of passage', crossing over (transition, change)

Arts of Civilization : *enaireacht*, fowling

DIVINATION SYMBOLISM.

Description : four long notches perpendicular across the stemline

Word Ogham (Morann mac Main) : "*Ergnaid fid*—distinguished wood; a name for the trembling tree"

Word Ogham (Mac Ind Oic) : "*Comainm carat*—synonym for *friend*"

Tarot Equivalent : The (Falling) Tower—false hopes, sudden changes, breakdown, limitations of clinging to the old

Ogham Lochlannach : *fehu*—physical power, possessions and prosperity; also 'wealth' or 'cattle'; ownership; also slavery, bondage; a valuable object

Personality : caring
  Inversion : insecure

Oracular Meaning : overcoming barriers and problems, facing fears, overcoming death (transition, change), working through emotional distress, overcoming doubts (misunderstanding), overcoming final obstacles toward completion

20. ioho — *yew tree*

"*Although all things are comprehended by the
Mind—yet the Dweller exists beyond the Mind.
The first mind is reason. The second is intuition.
Within the third dwells the pattern,
who is neither intellect nor inclination,
more excellent than all speech and notion.*"

—The Oracle of the Silent Yew
(Monroe Version)

An 'end-cycle' has been achieved. Death of the
old has made way for the new. The Seeker has
shed skin and rebirth into a new cycle awaits.
Yew represents the essence of the unadulter-
ated Self, fully defragmented, or at the very
least emerging onto a higher plane of realization and experience with the next cycle of the
pathway—the next ladder—that awaits us. A
sense of accomplishment is well-deserved, but
the the gateway to a complete Ascension is
still forthcoming.

ESOTERIC CORRESPONDENCE.

Alternate Names : idad, ida, ibur, ywen,
        iodha, idho, iubhar, uhr
Alphabet Letter : "I"/"J" and "Y"

Ogma's Tree : "Service-tree"

Alternate Trees : dogwood, cypress, hemlock

Bardic Value : 20; *red.* 2; or often unnum-
    bered

Forest Rank (British) : Bramble

Forest Rank (Irish) : Chieftain

Quadratic Element : Earth

Druid Guardian : Iachim

Celtic Deities : Arawn, Arianrhod, Dagda Mor,
    Samhann

Druidic Deities : Ith (towers and buildings),
    Ialonus (cultivated fields), Iorix
    (astronomy, meteors and space)

Solar Month : n/a

Lunar Month : Day before Winter Solstice

Color Ogham : *irfind*, very white, also dark
    green

Bird Ogham : *illait*, eaglet (courage, renewal)

Sacred Animal : spider (the gateway)

Sacred Gems : emerald, diamond, star-ruby

Ogham Forest Tract : poison, poisoned wea-
    pons, archery-bows

 Arts of Civilization : *iascaireacht*, fishing

DIVINATION SYMBOLISM.

Description : five long notches perpendicular
      across the stemline

Word Ogham (Morann mac Main) : "*Siniu
      fedaib*—oldest of woods; and *ibur*,
      a name for the service-tree"

Word Ogham (Mac Ind Oic) : "*Crinem feda*—
      most withered of wood, or sword,
      to wit, a service-tree"

Tarot Equivalent : Death—abrupt changes,
      letting go, transitions, unfortunate
      realizations; does not typically
      indicate 'physical body' death

Ogham Lochlannach : *Eihwaz*—life, death, the
      rebirth cycle; also 'Ingwaz' (deity)

Personality : enduring
 Inversion : sanguine

Oracular Meaning : completion, changes,
      renewal, transformation, forth-
      coming rebirth, the next step,
      the life and death cycle, infinity,
      immortality of the spirit

THE
ORACLE

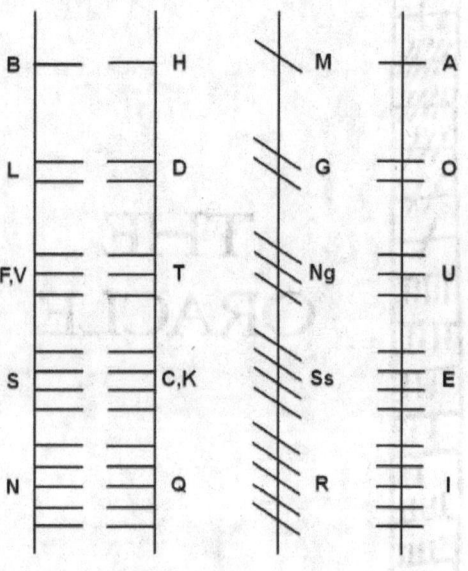

divination in the druidic tradition

"[Druid] systems of divination are rather different to many modern methods of 'fortunetelling'. They used divination techniques to learn the hidden secrets about things, so they could be just as interested in divining someone's secret past as in determining the future. They understood that by knowing someone's secret past, the future can be predicted with a great deal of precision..."
—Richard Webster
'Omens, Oghams & Oracles'

READING THE LAND.

During the early developmental period of the Mardukite Research Organization, the present author traveled over 20,000 miles on the American Greyhound bus lines in just a few short years—most of them exceptionally long trips crisscrossing the United States—even coast-to-coast. Rather than driving, this chance to ride passively as a passenger, journeying across the surface of the land, allowed for observation and interactions at new levels of realization.

Although the concept is alluded to in many manuals of 'earth mysticism', the experience afforded opportunities for "reading" the resonant energy of various regions and landscapes. It was curious to note that although state-lines are indeed purely "political" boundaries, there are observable differences when crossing either side of these thresholds. The land and those that dwell on it are indeed *one*, and they clearly have an influential effect on one another. All is connected together.

Although the manner of understanding the specific projected energies of life is difficult to instruct in a book, the interconnected lore of the Oghamic tradition does reflect this. An individual that is high in awareness can easily "tune in" to sense these "subtle energies. But, a person does not really have to be all that 'sensitive' to perceive that the 'feeling' of an oak forest is quite different than an aspen forest—or notice the distinguished presence (or 'aura') of a lone elm tree surrounded by a circle-grove of pines. A systematic understanding of these qualities allows a Druid (or similar practitioner) the ability to "read" the land, in a sense.

ORACLES & DIVINATION.

Divination is a personal individualized application of metaphysical systems or magical traditions—and the Ogham is certainly among the most individually personal and intuitive means of 'reading' the omens of life. Still, all methods of divination depend on the operator's (seer, medium, magician, Druid, diviner) relationship with the system itself (its meaning, symbolism) and the actual implements (tools, stones, sticks).

Although we find no shortage of lore, tales and stories within Celtic, Druid and Elven-Faerie systems—all of which reach into the ancient pools of knowledge—we are often at a loss for precise methods of divination and interpretation that are held completely and one-hundred percent 'authentic' to original source-cultures thousands of years ago.

There are no absolute standards or rules toward handling oracles and divination in the Druidic tradition as it is observed today. We have only suggestions. And magical practices must be personalized to a certain extent in order to be effective anyways.

THE CRANE BAG.

The divinatory "tools" employed for an oracle are generally treated as "sacred" items. They are usually kept hidden away from the eyes of the 'profane' or 'uninitiated' and are often quite personal possessions. The traditional Oghamancer's 'shamanic pouch' or 'medicine bag' serves this purpose for the Ogham sticks. Drawing *fews* from a pouch or bag also replaces the need to "shuffle" or randomize a card-based system. This bag may be shaken up and its contents could even be emptied out all at once if desired.

In one Druidic tradition, invention of the Ogham was inspired by observing flights of cranes, which "form the characters of the letters as they fly." The phrase *crane knowledge* came to denote the hidden knowledge that Oghamic tradition conceals—and that divination is thought to reveal.

A bag or pouch is traditionally used to hold and store a set of *Ogham sticks*. During an oracle reading, *fews* may be drawn individually from the bag—or the bag may be used to drop the entire set onto a 'spread'. But even a single *few* may be drawn for some quick overall insight.

PRAYERS & SILVER-BELLS.

Divination is connected to the "Other"—or else piercing the veils of mystery and not-knowing that enshroud knowledge that is considered "Divine" relative to material existence and the human condition. In Celtic cosmology, the "Other" is often treated literally as the "Otherworld," which includes the *'Realm of Faerie'*. Druids (and other similar practitioners) have maintained a long-standing connection to the "Otherworld."

One particular connection to the "Other" is represented by the *Ogham* tree most sacred to the Avalonian Druidesses—the Apple. Its wood is used to fashion a traditional tool called the "Silver Branch"—also known as *'craebh ciuil'* or "Poet's Branch" in the Bardic lore and Oghamic systems. This "wand" serves as a catalyst to bridge the transmission of energy and information between the "Other" and the medium or operator.

To construct the tool, attach silver bells to a single branch of apple wood, twelve to sixteen inches long. It may even be a forked branch or with smaller offshoots to provide nodes for attaching three bells with blue and white ribbon. According to traditional lore, the hanging bells are meant to represent apples themselves. Before any type of divination is performed, the bells would be rung three times in order to purify the 'air' and ensure an accurate reading. A prayer or invocation might also be spoken—such as:

Hail to thee, Ogma Sun-Face;
Watchful Eye of the Great God;
Seeing Eye of the God of Glory;
Witnessing Eye of the King of the Living.

Pour down and bestow your blessing;
Pour down and bestow your skill;
Pour down and bestow your power;
Unmask the God of Life for this divination.

oghamancy and the art of casting ogham fews

"In the 'Tochmarc Etain', the omen sticks are called 'eochra ecsi', or 'keys of knowledge'. The 'Senchus Mor' describes a type of judgment, used to find a murderer or thief, which is called 'crannchur', or 'casting the woods'.
J. A. MacCulloch says that some early Irish saints used a kind of divination called 'fidlanna', which used pieces of wood..."

—D.J. Conway
'By Oak, Ash & Thorn'

Twenty (or twenty-one, including a blank) *Ogham fews* serve as the variable elements of the Oghamic oracle system employed in modern 'New Age' practices. Use of *Ogham fews* for any divinatory purpose is subject to the interpretation of an Oghamancer (magician, Druid, practitioner, &tc.) that is familiar with those energies represented by the 'Green World' of the Forest Trees. As a result, the system is generally referred to as the 'Celtic Oracle of the Forest Trees' or else the 'Celtic Tree Oracle'.

SPREAD-CLOTHS & CASTING-CLOTHS.

A special surface area is used for divination that may or may not surround an 'altar'—depending on the tradition—but should be at least temporarily designated as oracular space with some kind of 'cloth' material, especially if working indoors. Sometimes the ground may be used outdoors, but it is still distinguished with some type pattern or "spread" to indicate its application to the oracle.

The 'cloth' could also be printed with the 'spread' symbolism, if desired. In either case, it is *on* this 'spread' which one *casts* the Ogham *fews* from the 'Crane Bag'. Alternatively, one could trace an area out with chalk or charcoal, if we're staying true to natural applications.

A "spread" is any oracular pattern used to 'read' or interpret the meaning of more than one facet randomly selected from a divination system; or more than one Ogham "*few*." The "spread" involves applying a preassigned meaning to specific placements or positions within the pattern.

Any divination system, such as the Ogham, tarot, runes and so forth, require a combination of two factors, or a meeting point of two axis: the fixed environment, and the variable elements. The "spread" provides a fixed environment or "setting" on which the "variables" (the Ogham *fews*) are "cast" or "set" out upon. The type or manner of "spread" used is indicative of the 'standard' by which the cosmos are seen from the point of view of the Observer or Diviner. A particular "spread" (or "layout"), or point-of-view, is selected based on the type of information an individual seeks to gain.

FORFEDHA—THE FIFTHS SPREAD.

An additional *aicme* of five Oghams appear in the *Book of Ballymote*—called the *Forfedha* or "*Fifths.*" They are traditionally not used as *Ogham sticks*, but are instead the symbols on which *Ogham fews* are cast as a "spread." Variations of interpretation occur throughout 'New Age' traditions.

The version provided here closely matches a system instructed to the present author during the 1990s. It has been since updated.

As was stated in the *Pheryllt Researches:**

> "As an Ogham oracle spread, the *Forfedha* are the fixed zones—a background matrix—on which the *fews* are variable elements. A combination of these two are what suggest the total 'reading'."

Some theorize that the *Forfedha* "Fifths" or 'Elemental/Directional' division used in the model represents the divisions of Ireland, and simultaneously, the Otherworld Kingdoms of Faerie (or presumably, the "Tuatha d'Anu"). For Ogham divination systems, the "Fifths" represent a microcosm of creation, a *spread* mirroring the cosmos. Continuing from the *Pheryllt Researches:*

> "*Forfedha* might be drawn on the ground before a sacred 'Oracle Tree', or imprinted on a 'board' or 'spread-cloth'. Design of this 'spread' should include a portion for each of the Four Directions, therefore the Four Elements, plus a 'center' area, which represents the 'fifth' position."

---

* Available as "*Draconomicon (Vol. 2): Pheryllt Researhes*" and in "*The Complete Book of Pheryllt*" (deluxe edition hardcover anthology).

In contrast to the traditional *fedha* or *fews*, there is marginal consistency between the various New Age interpretations of *forfedha*. Our *forfedha* model displayed here is based on a version of the Ogham 'scales' depicted in the *Book of Ballymote*. Four divisions are clearly visible, as is the "X" in the center. The image reproduced here features the remaining Ogham script as an ornamental addition, which is not required in your own graphic representation of the Fifths-Spread.

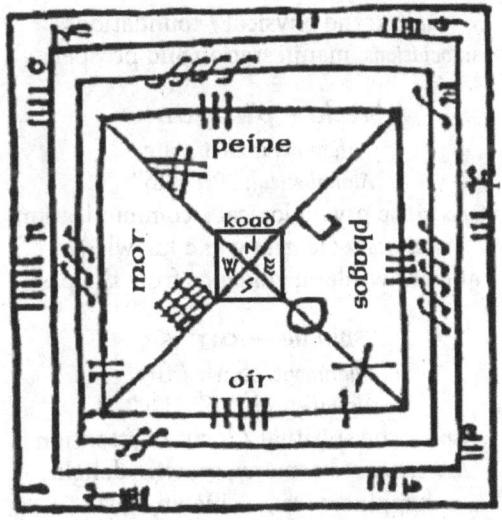

Interpretation of the *forfedha* given below is unique to this work—whereas other sources often designate different names and classifications, making any comparative research for this part quite difficult. Therefore, for this example, the present author relied on personal notebooks maintained in the 1990s for the *Elven-Druid* and *Pheryllt* systems.

*pine — **peine** %*
Alignment: north / earth
Alphabetical: "Pe" "Ui"
Aspect: the physical / foundations
Associations: manifestation and prosperity

*beech — **phagos** @*
Alignment: east / air
Alphabetical: "Ph" "Io"
Aspect: the psychological / communication
Associations: learning and knowledge;
ancient wisdom; guidance from the past

*spindle — **oir** ◇*
Alignment: south / fire
Alphabetical: "Oi" "Th"
Aspect: the spiritual / focus of attention
Associations: harmony; growth; delight;
happiness from achieving goals

the sea — mor
Alignment: west / water
Alphabetical: "Xi" "Ae"
Aspect: the emotional / influences
Association: challenges and turbulence;
imprinting; also journeys and travel

the grove — koaδ x
Alignment: center (middle) / spirit
Alphabetical: "Ch" "Ea"
Aspect: the Self / etheric link between all
Association: where all things are connected;
Alpha-Spirit and Spiritual Timeline
(True Knowledge across all 'lifetimes')

Creative interpretations are discerned by combining the general 'aura' gleaned from the Ogham *few*—as previously catalogued—with the situation or environment represented by its position in the spread. For example, depending on the question posed: *Birch ('beith')* might represent 'new beginnings and vitality'. If we consider what introducing 'new vitality' to 'challenges and conflict' (in the '*mor*' position) essentially is, it would be like "fanning flames"—yet, this same 'vitality' in 'learning' (the '*phagos*' position) could indicate "over-eagerness."

There are no definitive 'rules' for "casting" the *fews*. You might choose to select a stick individually from a 'crane bag' and place it in each position around the 'spread'. One might also gather the sticks in their hand and drop them onto the 'spread' surface from above—our simply pour them all out from a 'crane bag' and interpret how they land across the 'spread'. It might be that any or all of these is appropriate, but that a diviner's intuition will guide their perform- ance of divinatory actions by necessity.

If a diviner is pulling individual *fews* from a 'crane bag' to place onto the 'spread', there should be a sequential order for laying the *fews* down into positions. Traditionally, the energy-flow incited by such actions should follow a 'spiral-like' pattern—either toward or away from the center. For example, from *koad*, to *peine*, *phagos*, *oir* and *mor*. Or some diviner's might prefer another pattern.

As a divination system, Ogham requires a high level of intuition by practitioners, not to mention studying a language and style unfamiliar in a world of tarot and runes— but it doesn't have to be intimidating.

A CELTIC TREE ORACLE QUICK-START.

Although there is no substitute for intuitively understanding and applying the lore of the Green World to Ogham—as described throughout this present volume—the following 'New Age' interpretation from many decades ago may assist a beginner in 'jump-starting' their practical applications of the "Celtic Tree Oracle." This 'quick-start' list is only one possible way of interpreting the *Forfedha-Fifths-Spread* and is not a definitive standard that a reader 'must' adhere to. It simply suffices to at least get a Seeker moving in a practical direction.

1. BIRCH / *beith*
   in KOAD : new starts and beginnings
   in PEINE : fortune and riches
   in PHAGOS : youthful eagerness
   in OIR : turbulence and disturbance
   in MOR : new fanned fury (aggression)

2. ROWAN / *luis*
   in KOAD : protective (dominance)
   in PEINE : abundance and affluence
   in PHAGOS : new insight or discovery
   in OIR : productivity and advancement
   in MOR : overcoming adversity

3. ALDER / *fearn*
   in KOAD : fundamentals (basics)
   in PEINE : underlying challenges
   in PHAGOS : apathy or disinterest
   in OIR : overcoming doubts
   in MOR : acute vigilance

4. WILLOW / *saille*
   in KOAD : intuition or insight
   in PEINE : brooding or excess
   in PHAGOS : wit and cunning
   in OIR : passivity and femininity
   in MOR : securing the advantage

5. ASH / *nuin*
   in KOAD : world tree (seeking Infinity)
   in PEINE : loss (starting over)
   in PHAGOS : renewed interest
   in OIR : new influences or interests
   in MOR : mass gathering (abundance)

6. HAWTHORN / *huathe*
   in KOAD : weaknesses (integrity)
   in PEINE : shortage or poverty
   in PHAGOS : ignorance or stubbornness
   in OIR : disharmony or misfortune
   in MOR : defeat or sudden change

7. OAK / *duir*
   in KOAD : realizations and beliefs

in PEINE : security and restfulness
in PHAGOS : recognition and retention
in OIR : discontentment (change needed)
in MOR : destruction or overcoming

8. HOLLY / *tinne*
in KOAD : steadfastness or sternness
in PEINE : planning ahead (for harvest)
in PHAGOS : discernment (decisions)
in OIR : rejection and choices (action)
in MOR : revenge and retribution

9. HAZEL / *coll*
in KOAD : creativity and intuition
in PEINE : created goods and arts
in PHAGOS : teaching and instruction
in OIR : accomplishment (satisfaction)
in MOR : legal matters and judgment

10. APPLE / *quert*
in KOAD : perfection (beauty)
in PEINE : wholeness (duality)
in PHAGOS : occult knowledge
in OIR : rewards (harmony in life)
in MOR : mistrust and betrayal

11. VINE / *muin*
in KOAD : reserved (abstained)
in PEINE : class or prestige
in PHAGOS : moderation of intake

in OIR : shrewdness and subtlety
in MOR : boastful pride (excess)

12. IVY / *gort*
in KOAD : development (new skills)
in PEINE : restriction of growth
in PHAGOS : educational grades
in OIR : attainment and persistence
in MOR : ruin and stagnation

13. REED / *ngetal*
in KOAD : direct action (will)
in PEINE : etiquette and records
in PHAGOS : symmetry (cohesion)
in OIR : harmony (tranquility)
in MOR : stillness and inaction

14. BLACKTHORN / *straif*
in KOAD : stewardship (guarding)
in PEINE : favors and debts owed
in PHAGOS : tests (of the true Self)
in OIR : violent (passionate)
in MOR : capture and imprisonment

15. ELDER / *ruis*
in KOAD : maturity and age
in PEINE : sharing and generosity
in PHAGOS : progress and advancement
in OIR : new information (rethinking)
in MOR : survivalism (quest for Infinity)

16. FIR / *ailim*
   in KOAD : objectivity ('high views')
   in PEINE : individuality and singularity
   in PHAGOS : accomplishment
   in OIR : discovery (magnification)
   in MOR : strategy (perspective/POV)

17. FURZE / *ohn*
   in KOAD : collected wisdom
   in PEINE : collected wealth
   in PHAGOS : collected knowledge
   in OIR : collected authority
   in MOR : collected experience

18. HEATHER / *ur*
   in KOAD : new inspiration (sources)
   in PEINE : greed and obsession
   in PHAGOS : zealousness (tenacious)
   in OIR : disturbance (fragmentation)
   in MOR : raging tides (before the calm)

19. ASPEN / *eadha*
   in KOAD : overcoming (success)
   in PEINE : effort (to complete actions)
   in PHAGOS : structure and discipline
   in OIR : overcoming all effort-force
   in MOR : force applied (to cause action)

20. YEW / *ioho*
   in KOAD : rebirth (eternity or Infinity)

in PEINE : grief (losses along the way)
in PHAGOS : disillusionment (clarity)
in OIR : discordance or disharmony
in MOR : fear (of unknown/next steps)

CLASSICS OF MARDUKITE MESOPOTAMIA
REVISED HARDCOVER 2-VOLUME SET

SUMERIAN RELIGION

Introducing the Anunnaki Gods
of Mesopotamian Neopaganism

Mardukite Liber-50

by Joshua Free

BABYLONIAN MYTH & MAGIC

Spiritual Traditions and Mysticism
in Mesopotamian Anunnaki Religion

Mardukite Liber-51+E

by Joshua Free

SYSTEMOLOGY BASICS HARDCOVER SET

THE POWER OF ZU

Applying Mardukite Zuism and
Systemology to Everyday Life
Systemology Liber-S1-Z
based on a lecture series
by Joshua Free

THE WAY INTO THE FUTURE

A Handbook for the New Human
Systemology Liber-S1-W
collected works mini-anthology
by Joshua Free

SYSTEMOLOGY
The Pathway to Self-Honesty

GO FURTHER AND BE

CRYSTAL CLEAR

JOSHUA FREE

CRYSTAL CLEAR

(Handbook for Seekers)

Mardukite Systemology Liber-2B
by Joshua Free

Take control of your destiny
and chart the first steps
toward your own spiritual evolution.
Realize new potentials of the
Human Condition with
a Self-guiding handbook for
Self-Processing toward
Self-Actualization
in Self-Honesty using actual
techniques and training
provided for the coveted
"Mardukite Systemology Grade-III
Self-Defragmentation Course Program"
—once only available
directly and privately from
the underground Systemology Society.

Discover the amazing power behind the
applied spiritual technology
used for counseling and advisement in
the tradition of Mardukite Zuism.

JOSHUA FREE

PUBLISHED BY THE **JOSHUA FREE** IMPRINT REPRESENTING

The Founding Church of Mardukite Zuism

THE JOSHUA FREE IMPRINT
JFI PUBLICATIONS

MARDUKITE
ZUISM

mardukite.com

www.ingramcontent.com/pod-product-compliance
Lightning Source LLC
Chambersburg PA
CBHW011238120626
46549CB00009B/3316

* 9 7 9 8 9 8 7 1 2 4 9 5 6 *